FOR OUR CHILDREN

FOR OUR CHILDREN

A DIFFERENT APPROACH TO PUBLIC EDUCATION

Frank Macchiarola
and Thomas Hauser

CONTINUUM · NEW YORK

1985
The Continuum Publishing Company
370 Lexington Avenue, New York, N.Y. 10017

Library of Congress Cataloging in Publication Data

Macchiarola, Frank J.
    For our children.

    1. Public schools—United States.   2. Education
and state—United States.   I. Hauser, Thomas.
II. Title.
LA217.M25 1985   379.73   84-23008
ISBN 0-8264-0356-5

Good educators make a difference. We dedicate this book to the following teachers, who taught us, cared about us, and gave us much of what we have today. Some are deceased. We've been long separated from others. They are heroes who set a standard we would wish for children in school everywhere:

Thomas Duffy
Ronald Edmonds
Joseph A. Ellis
James J. Flynn
John Greany
Brother Brendan Irwin, F.S.C.
Clement Jedrzejewski
Howard Lilienthal
Dwight Miner
Richard Morgan
Thomas Rock
Janet Rogowsky
David B. Truman
Richard Uviller
Bessie Whalley

Contents

Foreword

Education has to be at the top of everyone's priority list in or out of government. The future of our nation is dependent on better educated children who can secure the new jobs which are so much more complicated because of the new technology.

When I became the mayor of New York City on January 1, 1978, one of the first matters before me was the appointment of a new chancellor to run the largest public school system in the world. Our Board of Education is comprised of seven members, only two of whom are appointed by the mayor, and it is they who select the chancellor by majority vote. Therefore, the mayor's involvement in selecting the chancellor is far less by direction than by persuasion.

I recruited Frank Macchiarola as a candidate for the job of chancellor. My support of him was opposed by the head of the United Federation of Teachers, Al Shanker. I remember Al Shanker telling me that he had more than a majority of the votes necessary to elect the new chancellor and that the new chancellor would be someone he proposed rather than someone I chose. I surprised not only him but everyone else when as a result of my persuasion I secured the votes on the Board necessary to effectuate the election of Frank as chancellor. I believe in retrospect that it is now nearly the unanimous view that he is one of the greatest, if not the greatest, of all the chancellors that the City of New York has ever had. His accomplishments are enormous. Indeed, Al Shanker subsequently advised me that I was right in pressing for his appointment and that he had been wrong to oppose him.

What is it that Frank Macchiarola did in the five years that he was chancellor? He did what a chancellor should do. He lead, inspired, implemented, innovated, and pressed successfully all the other institutions the Board of Education must have on their side to function well. His watchword was "every child can learn," and as a result of his efforts, the children of the City of New York read, write, and do math much better than they did before he came. He set new plateaus upon which to build. Instead of reading below the national norm, as they did when Frank began, our children now read above the national average and have done so for the last four years. Our children also have done math for the last three years above the national average.

I believe that public service is the noblest of professions if it is done honestly and done well. Frank Macchiarola performed a marvelous service and will always be remembered as the modern-day chancellor who reversed a declining public school system in New York City and gave it new hope. I recommend to you the book he has written with Thomas Hauser, *For Our Children*. It is important because it sets the agenda for the future.

EDWARD I. KOCH
MAYOR OF NEW YORK

1

The Need for Reform

That the United States is currently engaged in a national debate over public education is hardly surprising. America has long used its public schools as an instrument for shaping society, and loud, sometimes violent dissent has often accompanied that process. In an effort to resolve our three-hundred-year-old racial problems, we integrated public schools through judicial decisions and court orders. In response to hunger and malnutrition, we inaugurated school breakfast and lunch programs. So that students could better cope with changing social mores, we brought sex education into the classroom. Prayer has been shuttled in and out of the nation's schools. Each of these measures and others like them divided America. Today, though, there is one belief that has united the nation: the belief that our public schools are no longer educating students properly.

Too many of our children are being failed by the system. Our schools are producing students who cannot read adequately, think clearly, or do basic arithmetic. The quality of a high school diploma is no longer what it used to be, and evidence of that failure surrounds us.

On any given day, 25 percent of the students in Boston's junior high school system are absent. More than half of the students who matriculate in Chicago's public high schools fail to graduate. The national high school dropout rate is close to 25 percent, and despite massive proof to the contrary, there is a widely held notion that certain classes of children are not educable. Given the poor quality of instruction and the hopelessness apparent in many school settings, educators cannot credibly ask students to stay in the classroom simply as a convenient way to keep them off the streets. Thus, alongside the notable examples of success that exist in public schools stand the millions of students who have been failed by the system.

Recent studies indicate that almost one-fifth of all eighteen-year-olds in the United States are functionally illiterate. Reading is the most important educational skill a child can acquire. It opens the door to vast enrichment and knowledge. In our society, without the ability to read it is impossible to capitalize on the resources that America has to offer. For a country that promises a public school education to all its citizens, for a country that sees a high school diploma as the minimum educational requirement for most employment, these statistics are appalling.

Even those who, on balance, are satisfied with our nation's schools concede that things simply aren't happening the way they should. There was a time when college deans could greet each successive freshman class with the exhortation that, academically, they were the best incoming class ever; that their entrance examination scores were remarkably high; that they had broken all the records. It's been years since we've been able to say that to students. Even the notion that there is an age for compulsory education in this country has been exposed as myth. All an observer need do is walk the streets of virtually any community during school hours to see ten-and twelve-year-olds, unattended, ripe for exploitation, forgotten.

America cannot be great if its public schools continue to turn out, as graduates or as dropouts, students who are functionally illiterate. The failure to educate has weakened our nation. It has left our work force ill-prepared to contend with competition from abroad. It has led, in many places, to a horribly defeatist attitude toward public education—particularly in urban areas, where many families at all socioeconomic levels have abandoned the public schools in favor of private institutions because they simply don't think public schools can do an adequate job.

We believe that the decline in American public education is a tragedy. Public schools are at the core of American democracy, and without a strong, vibrant system of public education, future generations will experience "the American dream" as a mirage. But the vitality of America's public schools can be restored if we as a people are willing to commit ourselves to their improvement.

American public education is built upon an assumption that, by world standards, is quite rare—the assumption that schools should educate *all* of the children, and do so in approximately the same manner for each child. In other industrialized nations, a substantial number of students are removed from academic tracks early in their schooling. By contrast, in the United States, "tracking" —a system that puts students in classes based on their achievement and potential academic ability—is less severe, and some college experience is regarded as the goal of the "average" child. This undertaking is based on a courageous optimism regarding the capacity of children and involves the expenditure of over $130 billion annually on public education.

Historically, school has been the avenue of upward mobility for our poor and minority peoples. It has assimilated our immigrant forebears into American society, while enabling them to hold on to their unique cultural and ethnic heritage. Of all public institutions, it is our schools that possess the greatest potential for eliminating class differences, bringing together rich and poor in their formative years. And, if our schools have often been the focus of conflict and debate, it is because they reflect our differences as a society; because they pass on our central values as people from one generation to another.

There has been much talk lately, particularly in America's cities, about saving the schools for the middle class. We find the implications inherent in such dialogue particularly distressing. All of our children are of the same class in that they share the common goal of a successful future. And though our schools—urban, suburban, and rural— are remarkably diverse, far more unites than divides them.

We are totally committed to seeing that each child leaves our public school system fully literate and with the skills needed to survive. This means that every student should be able to read, write, compute, understand abstract principles, and possess a certain level of accumulated wisdom and knowledge. Moreover, we expect each student who graduates to be capable of performing in an adult role and to appreciate the meaning of work. All too often, our schools fail at these tasks and, in so doing, they have crushed the dreams and limited the reasonable expectations of our children.

In writing this book, we hope to influence a broad spectrum of Americans. We are telling you—the informed public—that certain things have to be understood about the condition of our schools, and that certain steps must be taken to improve them. We hope to enlighten those who know little or nothing about public education and motivate you, the reader, to become involved. We will offer clear choices to policy-makers. And we intend to give pause to those who look at educational reform simply as another way to pump more money into public schools without regard to accountability and standards. We will identify what attributes school systems need in order to be effective. And we will do this consistent with a set of fundamental principles, which are as follows:

1. All children can learn.
2. All children are equal.
3. It is the responsibility of the public school
system to promote learning and equality for all children.

Some of the problems we address have been touched on in reports by others. Within the past few years, more than a dozen serious and scholarly studies critical of American public education have been published, and in many respects these publications are admirable. However, the overwhelming majority have been prepared with the heavy involvement and support of those with special interests in the process of education—professional educators at the high school and university level, teachers union officials, state and local political appointees. They focus on more daily hours in class, greater rigor in subject matter, higher teacher salaries, the upgrading of math and science instruction, and a longer school year. There has been talk of increased requirements for teachers, but the impact of educational reform upon those already teaching has been blunted by the politics of past reform. The reports embrace too many remedies and make too many recommendations without a sense of what should come first. They look at schools in traditional terms without focusing on urgently needed structural changes. And save for the prospect of significantly increased taxes to pay for reform, adults other than teachers have been spared new obligations. Although some reform of school practice will be effected by these solutions, we suggest that the focus of the reform movement to date has been too severely restricted and almost mechanical in its attitude toward children. It has ignored areas where reform should take place and will result in the same old—and ineffective—solutions of spending away a problem. Indeed, the clearest example of the mismatch between what students need and what they are being offered comes in various proposals to lengthen the school day and extend the school year. Given the present level of high school dropouts and chronic absenteeism, such a "reform" simply offers more of what students have already rejected. Unless the dialogue of reform is broadened to include improved school practices, stronger school management, and broader participation in schooling by citizens excluded from the process, effective change will not occur.

We are not "outsiders" to public education. Indeed, one of us—an optimist with the belief that children can be well served by public schools—was chancellor of the New York City school system for five years. And during those years, for the first time in more than a decade, the effectively measured reading and math skills of New York City's children rose above the national norm. Yet despite, or perhaps because of, that experience, we start out with a firm belief that real reform for education cannot come from within the educational establishment. The establishment has a commitment to what is, and not enough understanding of what *can be*. Professional educators are too strongly affected by the process of education and rarely confront its product. Too few teachers and administrators see the dropout—the student failed by the system. And too few teachers and administrators know what skills high school graduates ought to possess. Too often, their understanding of children is limited to students who come to school. They ignore those who do not. They are bound by an often outmoded curriculum, usually quite similar to what they studied when they went to school. They tend to regard education as the exclusive province of educators and see solutions within terms of a purely academic strategy. They do not understand management. They believe, basically, that what they teach is more important than what students learn. They do not realize that, if children are to become adult producers of ideas, goods, and services rather than recipients of government largesse, the focus of public education must be on what students are capable of achieving *after* they leave school. These educators overlook ways in which other institutions can be brought into the reform process and thereby minimize the impact of outside groups in restructuring and redesigning schools. They tend to close ranks in defensive fashion and look at education as their business and their business alone.

Real reform of America's public schools must come

with the direct assistance and involvement of people out-side the school system; people who know the outside world and have a stake in students as fellow workers and colleagues; people who are not satisfied with the quality of today's schools. Parents, state and local officials, and America's business community must all become part of the process. Their intervention is essential to meaningful reform, and there will be very little basic reform until the dominance of the insiders is overcome.

Indeed, in recent years, the two most significant causes of positive change in American education have come as the result of pressure from outside of school systems, not pressure from within. The first of these—the movement back to basics—was forced upon schools by discontent among business leaders and state legislators. Questioning the integrity of the high school diploma, they fought for minimum standards of student skill and forced compe-tency examinations as a condition to high school diplomas in approximately forty states. They did so against the near unanimous opposition of the educational community. Yet, even with the deficiencies inherent in minimum com-petency testing—and there are several—such an emphasis has resulted in strengthened curriculum and increased ed-ucational standards.

The second movement—the push for tuition tax cred-its—has reminded educators that, unless public schools improve, the public will turn to private institutions to ed-ucate its children. These institutions, with less than one-tenth the enrollment of public schools, have been historically important in providing competition to strengthen the public school system, and it is clear that there is no longer any such thing as a student who has to attend public school. Even among the disadvantaged and poor, the search for options has begun. In cities such as Philadelphia, Boston, Newark, and New York, almost half the children in Catholic parochial schools are black and Hispanic—and many of these children are not Catholic. The tuition tax credit movement threatens public schools with loss of enrollment, and loss of enrollment threatens loss of jobs. The willingness of teachers and other educators to consider new strategies for school improvement is related in part to a realization of their own self-interest. Unless public education regains a measure of public support and begins to prosper, these teachers and educators will lose their jobs.

In sum, reform must be imposed upon school systems; and it must concentrate on what schools are to *accomplish*—not what they are to spend. Indeed, we would go so far as to say that true reform can never be led by those who work within school systems, because most educators insist that improved performance in school is almost wholly dependent upon the receipt of additional resources—more money, more support, more of what drives up the cost of providing services. They fail to focus on outcomes—what standards must be met, what students can achieve. They are blind to the fact that most of what has to be done does not require additional funds, but rather a change in work habits and attitudes toward children.

Public education in this country is in serious trouble, but its problems are not insoluble. Good school systems are rare. However, even in the most deprived urban neighborhoods, we can point to individual public schools led by brilliant educators that are successful and function well. What is needed, then, is to refocus and broaden the debate over American public education. And we will begin that process by examining a group of individuals too often ignored in discourse about our public schools—America's children.

2

The Plight of Children

This is a book about children—youngsters in school, and youngsters who leave school. We have to examine whether our system of public education meets the needs of these youngsters.

In many respects, children are treated differently today from the way they were treated twenty or thirty years ago because the society from which they come has changed. Even with recent increases in spending for education, America is in an age of diminished government commitment to social programs. It is an era of retrenchment, marked by "the politics of blame." Even in the nation's most liberal enclaves, victims are censured for their condition.

No school system exists apart from its environment. And like any area of public policy, educational reform must adapt to change. Yet most current policies regarding public education operate with an incomplete view of what it is that has happened to children and what children need.

We believe that too many children are not valued by parents or by society and therefore are not given responsible roles to play; that they are not told what is expected of them; that they drift from childhood through adolescence. Their feelings of powerlessness and lack of self-worth affect their behavior and limit their future. The reasons for the diminished status of children are many and varied. Because of our anxiety about the present and future, because of material pressures, because of the loss of hope and love in some sectors of society, and because of selfishness, it is clear that children have suffered. The role of schools must be considered within the context of a society where support systems for children are failing. And the task of public education must be seen as more formidable than ever, because children are given less support and less encouragement in their daily lives.

It used to be that American society invested in children. Parents had six or seven children, who would work at part-time jobs by age fourteen and would care for parents in their old age. America's children were a principal investment. The country sacrificed for its children because those children represented the future. Although the nation passed through an era when children were exploited and child labor laws became necessary, the period after the Great Depression was marked by great care for children. A child was an important economic asset as well as a human being to be loved.

Children today are too often seen as without value. Often, they are neglected and abused. Child protection agencies in this country report 750,000 cases of child abuse annually. Yet these same agencies often fail to act courageously to remove children from home settings that are destructive. The very value of life appears to have lessened. Almost half of all pregnancies in American cities terminate in abortion—a statistic that speaks volumes regardless of how one views a woman's right to control her own reproductive process. Threats of nuclear holocaust fill the air. Children realize that their lives could end at any moment even though they have done nothing wrong. They are frightened by a world order that promotes the proliferation of nuclear weapons regardless of the stakes involved. How does society teach a child to be respectful and caring in a world that seems to glorify violence; when the very existence of the planet is placed second to the question of which side in the Cold War has more and better weapons capable of destroying us all? To many children, it must seem as though chance has more to do with survival than does "rational, thinking man."

Children are unprotected people. They are undeveloped and insecure, innocent and pure, badly in need of support from their elders. Yet we live in an age when support systems for children are failing. Within the family, there has been a startling transformation over a short period of time. Between 1950 and 1980, the percentage of children from one-parent households has risen from 10 to 25. Far more children come from single-parent homes now than before. Many mothers are children themselves—fourteen or fifteen years old—who cannot adequately care for or guide themselves, let alone others. Family size has been reduced. And although this, in and of itself, is not a problem, the result has been that there are fewer instances of interaction between children and caring adults, such as uncles and aunts—particularly since the percentage of women who work full time has grown. Family interaction is important. It enables children to share ideas and explore the world with adults who are sympathetic and understanding. The extended family is an important teaching instrument for a child. Yet at the same time that public agencies have increased services to children, those that are provided at home have substantially declined. Twenty years ago, teachers knew that when a problem arose at school they could always reach a parent at work or at home, and that they could explain the situation in terms of standard notions of right and wrong. Now, in too many instances, schools have limited access, at best, to parents, and the understanding of what is good and proper for children has changed.

The role and authority of religious institutions in children's lives has also diminished. Adolescent drug use of epidemic proportions has reduced the capacity of youngsters, damaged their sense of worth, and lessened their potential as productive beings. "Social drug use" among children is widely accepted by some parents, who ignore the law and medical evidence that these drugs are damaging. Given present levels of technology, health care for the young is mediocre to poor. Too often—and particularly in urban areas—access to medical treatment is denied children who live virtually next door to our nation's most modern medical research centers.

A child who has difficulty seeing the chalkboard and is unable to focus on a printed page because of bad eyesight or dyslexia will, by definition, be slow to read. A child who, because of impaired hearing, cannot hear what a teacher is saying, what the teacher is asking and directing, will be unable to perform. That child is not being disobedient or flouting authority. That child is simply not receiving the message and is unable to respond.

One does not expect city sanitation workers, without help from the community, to keep streets clean. Streets will be clean only if citizens put their garbage in trash receptacles and incinerators. No one would suggest that the police alone can stop all crime; or that fire fighters can prevent all fire damage. Similarly, there is no way that public schools can educate and prepare students for adulthood without help from the outside.

They try. Public schools are cleaner and safer than the homes many of their students live in. Some children eat their best and most nutritious meal of the day in school. In many instances, during the worst days of winter, children remain in school after classes have ended to stay warm for as long as the custodial staff allows. Often, school administrators oppose the shutdown of schools during winter storms because of the shelter their schools afford.

In sum, many youngsters find that the adults most interested in promoting their well-being are in the schools. But even the most dedicated teachers and administrators find it hard to function in the face of a world that seemingly cares little for children, is indifferent at best, and often hostile. And, no matter what schools do, there is always the need for more. Students come to school without clear-cut moral values, and it is school that must help to fill the void. If a young child's parents work from nine to five, the school must stay open and care for that child beyond three in the afternoon. It cannot assume that the child will be well supervised at home. It cannot send latch-key children off to be cared for, as studies show they are, by siblings too young to assume adult roles.

The point is this: children now need additional care. And, if school expenditures are to be increased, they must be increased to meet this need. To date, the dialogue of reform has been sadly misfocused. Stimulated by teachers unions and other members of the education establishment, it has been built around higher costs for more services of the kind already provided. It has neglected the need for different services, such as school health care and after-school recreational programs. But children need these new services and a number of other things *from schools* because their circumstances at home and within society at large have changed.

The rules of the game have also changed. It used to be that a child's parents would come into school and say, "This is my child"; that religious institutions would lay down laws for personal conduct; that society would say, "We will stand and salute the flag because it is an important thing to do." Now the relationship between family, church, society, and child is marked by often conflicting signals. Some laws and regulations treat students as subject to almost absolute parental control. Even inoculations—mandated by federal law—require parental consent. In some cases, youngsters who want to be inoculated in order to satisfy federal requirements and thereby stay in school have been barred from classes because their parents did not authorize school officials to innoculate them. Yet, in other situations, the same parents and children are treated as separate entities. Take, for example, the matter of a school counselor who refers students to an abortion clinic. School officials in some jurisdictions are precluded from even telling a child's parents about the situation. Thus, on the one hand, children can't get innoculations without parental approval despite the fact that virtually everyone agrees innoculations are good. Yet with regard to an abortion—where there really is a difference of opinion—children are told they are free of their parents, they are their own masters. These are signals that children cannot clearly understand.

What we have, then, is a situation where children feel less certain of their place in society than in years past, and simultaneously, the support systems that society once offered are failing. In short, the condition of America's school-age children has changed. And, particularly in our cities, students have changed in one other respect as well—they are darker; they are black and yellow and brown.

There is, in some circles, a tendency to identify poor educational performance in our schools with a changing clientele—as if a high percentage of minority students serves to free educators from responsibility. Instead of promoting the idea that more help is needed for certain students, this brand of thinking has been used to explain that the needy cannot learn. It takes the burden of accountability off the shoulders of professional educators and is tantamount to writing off the poor. It ignores the realities of life in America's underclass. It is wrong.

A school system that is functioning properly can educate any child. Indeed, children of the poor can take far more from school than children of the rich because, often, their needs are greater. The poorer and more disadvantaged a student is, the greater the potential impact of school upon that child.

For a long time, academic studies "beat up" on disadvantaged youngsters, and too many educators brought despair to their schools by concluding that outside forces such as race and class were more important than factors within the school in determining whether students could master basic skills. There was an attitude that inner-city children wouldn't accept learning; that we couldn't expect students with poor socioeconomic backgrounds to perform; that certain children simply weren't meant for school, and professional educators could not be expected to solve their problems.

That attitude was, and remains, wrong. Effective instruction can take place with any student in any school. The task is not easy, particularly in ghetto areas where many students come to school believing that they cannot perform. They believe that society has deprived them of equal opportunity and destined them to lives of poverty. They do not feel welcome in the classroom; they don't see school as a place that is helpful to them. But the key to student learning is what goes on in school. Good educators know that it is they who control the destiny of students in their classrooms. They know that schools are institutions with the potential to move children out of bad circumstances into a good future. And they know that many schools have already met with success in educating youngsters from poor families by concentrating on what children are capable of becoming, not on what is wrong with them.

This is not to say that a good education will guarantee success. Our society is such that race, class, and other variables often conspire to prevent people of equal talent from achieving equal goals. But of all institutions, it is public education that best enhances the ability of America's underclass to perform. And given this reality, America cannot tolerate a philosophy that excuses professionals from educating all of our children. Nor can it tolerate a strategy to "save the schools" for the middle class. Such a strategy would be fundamentally flawed, because it presumes that certain children are more desirable than others. It presumes that it is the job of the school system to pick and choose from among those citizens who come to it which ones will be favored, based on their parents' economic status. The ultimate result of an educational program that tilts its benefits toward middle-class students is that no youngsters receive justice. Some are deprived of equality; others are given more than they deserve. You cannot have that in a system that promises to educate because, if that system is founded on the belief that some children are better than others, that system is no longer a *public* school system. Facing up to this issue—with an educational strategy designed to serve rich *and* poor—is the single most important item on the agenda of today's educators; it is also perhaps the most difficult item to achieve.

We return, then, to the three basic principles mentioned earlier: (1) all children can learn; (2) all children are equal; and (3) it is the responsibility of the public school system to promote learning and equality for all children. Each child will have different needs, but all children should be equal in the matter of entitlement. They are entitled to develop their capacity to the fullest extent possible, and it is the obligation of our public schools to share in that mission of fulfillment. These rights come with citizenship; they are secured by the Constitution and by the tradition of public schooling in America. Each child should get as much education as he or she can absorb in preparation for adulthood. And, once this is understood, the inevitable next step is the realization that we are not talking only about poor children or minority children or city children, but about *all* children.

There is a fundamental debate among educators as to whether schools should address all of the problems of children in society or focus on a narrower view of education. Those who adopt the expansive position feel that schools have a primary responsibility for moving students toward adulthood and caring for children's needs. Those who hold to a more restrictive view argue that schools cannot do more than they have traditionally done—particularly in the face of circumstances that make even the teaching of basic skills more difficult now than before. We support the former view. If changing family structures and other external factors mean that children's needs are not met at home, then schools must do the job. They did so during the early years of this century—when American educators made a conscious, sustained effort to assimilate the children of immigrants into the nation—and the results were positive. It can be done again. Educators can no longer focus solely on what goes on inside the classroom. More than ever, they must assume the role of teaching youngsters what it means to be a capable adult. The condition of children requires this expanded role.

The world has changed. Many presumptions that existed in years past are no longer valid. Once it was assumed that some youngsters would go through high school and college, and those who dropped out without a diploma would find reasonably profitable blue-collar jobs. No more! Yet schools have not adjusted to this transformation of the American economy. Not only have they failed to adjust to the plight of the dropout—they have failed to adjust to changing conditions that face high school *graduates* as well.

Schools continue to tell children, "Stay in school; you

will get a job." Yet many students who need jobs and would stay in school to get them know from the experience of relatives and friends that youngsters who stay in school don't necessarily find employment. Youngsters may not know the statistics of teenage unemployment, but they know the condition. What students worry about most—their future—is something that schools seem to pay the least attention to. Schools continue to say, "Do this today, do that tomorrow, and your future will fall into place." But students see that doing what they're supposed to do does little to guarantee that their future is assured. They know that school systems have not tried very hard to tie them into the job market, and that many educators are unaware of what students need in order to be gainfully employed.

Children aren't stupid. They understand the difference between what is promised and what is delivered. In many areas of the country—particularly in cities—youngsters see a flourishing underground economy. They see others their own age earning a substantial livelihood from running numbers and selling drugs. Thus, the student who stays in school knows, first, that the likelihood of getting a good job after graduating is not all that high and, second, that there are alternatives to education and an honest job. These children need more than talk to keep them in school. They need reasons based on reality. They need a commitment by schools and society to get them jobs, and they need the skills that will allow them to hold jobs.

The gap between what students need from a diploma and what they actually get has yet to be dealt with honestly and directly by educators. Instead, we have allowed a "blame the child" theory to permeate our educational system. Schools now view too many of their students as problems—problems who interfere with proper functioning of the school. If we truly care about children, our schools must reassess that view—and then decide what the basic unmet needs of children are. What we believe will be found is that children need a better break than they're getting. They need more encouragement and support from the adults in their lives. In many instances, they need simple human contact and love. Other times, they need to be taught the difference between right and wrong, good and bad. These are critical needs, often lacking in today's children. And, if unavailable elsewhere, they must be provided for in school.

We live in an age when our faith in fundamental values has been sorely tested. No longer are we told that succeeding generations of Americans are walking hand-in-hand with a confident view of what life is about, and how one ought to respect the basic institutions that make up our world. Yet the values upon which public schools should be built are quite basic, and the essential principle is that of justice.

The right to education is the right to a *good* education. Our schools must take all of America's children to the top of the mountain and show them what lies beyond. Rather than think we must push students to the limit of their capacity to learn, we must adopt the view that there are *no limits* on a child's ability to learn. Often, the improbable is possible.

In many respects American society has failed both its children and its schools. But justice will not permit us to point a finger at the wrongdoer and thereby discharge our responsibility to the wronged. If schools today are asked to do more than in the past—and to do it with less—then they must do more. And they can. Schools have the capacity to deliver quality education to all of our children—not only through the expenditure of more money but, more important, through better use of resources already at hand. The real question is whether today's educators care enough to do their job well. Much depends on the outcome of that issue. For America's children are our future, and whether they grow up to become responsible adults who contribute to society or unproductive individuals who weigh it down will be determined in large measure by what transpires during the next decade in our public schools.

3

The Powers That Be

We believe that school systems should be built on behalf of children, and that a school's primary focus should be on those youngsters. What is good for children? What do they need in a given situation? Again and again we come back to the fundamental operating principle that children must come first. If their needs increase, then schools by necessity must do more. If grown-ups are inconvenienced, if adults have to adjust their schedules to meet the needs of children, then so be it.

In public schools today, however, it is clear that many people who should be serving children serve only themselves. Not enough educators are concerned with shaping the lives of the next generation. Vested interests compete for expenditures, and special programs become ends in themselves rather than means to a desired end. Despite the hard work and dedication of many individuals, "the system" acts to frustrate educators and reduces their capacity to help children.

Good school systems require quality leadership, committed teachers, and a sense of mission. However, these requisites are often unappreciated by the forces that control public education. Political issues, budget cutbacks, union demands, and a host of other factors adversely influence what goes on in public schools. And before a program for reform is discussed, it is necessary to understand the power relationships that govern schools.

Federal and State Governments

Politics determines the allocation of government resources, and it is no secret that the operation of public schools is part of the political process. Under any model, schools are regulated by politicians, and politicians have an obligation to make sure that schools function properly. Yet overall—not just in the schools—government services have grown more costly and foundered badly.

Private industry models are not always appropriate for comparison with the public sector, but there is no denying that private industry must be cost-effective in order to survive. By contrast, the business of government goes on regardless of efficiency, and many services are provided almost without regard to productivity and cost. Government systems are far too slow in changing with the technology and art of the times. And rarely do they establish appropriate standards to monitor the quality of services provided. Rather, the budget process too often involves appropriation without evaluation of how well moneys previously appropriated were spent. There is a built-in constituency to continue spending as before. Unlike the private sector—where the purchasers' payment determines whether a service continues—with government, recipients often continue to get a service whether they want it or not.

This is not to say that government should abandon its

role in public education. To the contrary, that role is essential and must be preserved. But federal and state governments have not developed appropriate and clear roles within education. Legislative mandates and mandates by administrative agencies are frequently drafted because of lobbyist pressures and without appropriate consideration of the consequences. Often, these guidelines are in conflict with one another, with no rules for conflict resolution readily available. Local officials are frequently confused as to what superior governments expect of them. Too little attention is paid by government to the results of education—what students learn. Instead, the primary focus is on how much money goes into the educational process and who determines how it is spent. There are far too many regulations governing public education today and far too few standards.

During the fifty-year period from 1930 to 1980, local government's share of educational expenditures fell from 82.7 percent to 43.4 percent nationwide. State government expenditures increased from 16.9 percent to 46.8 percent. The federal government's share rose from a meager .4 percent to 9.8 percent of all public school funding. These trends will be subject to fluctuation in the years ahead, given changing economic conditions and the rapid growth of America's dependent population. Shifting age demographics have increased the competition for resources between young and old. Senior citizens—unlike children—can vote and, if the elderly and the young do battle, federally backed school expenditures may decline. Still, as demonstrated by the figures above, the change in public education from a basically local enterprise to a far more complex state and national undertaking has been profound. And, in the years to come, a major role for federal and state governments in funding education and thereby controlling to a degree what goes on in schools will undoubtedly remain. Thus, we must examine what that role is and should be.

Since the late 1950s—the time of the first Sputnik-era expenditures for math and science programs—federal intervention in public schools has grown. Yet, in retrospect, it is clear that this involvement has not always been accompanied by good judgment, and too often federal promises to local school districts have proved illusory. We believe that there is too much of a federal role in education and that, whenever possible, educational issues should be dealt with at a local level. However, there are several critical federal obligations.

The most important responsibility of the federal government in the educational arena is the enforcement of individual rights. We are talking now about federal guarantees that flow from the United States Constitution and Bill of Rights—due process, equal protection, free speech, and the like. It is an important role that goes to the heart of individual entitlements in a free society.

Second, the federal government is responsible for the formulation of a national education policy. Without this undertaking, a national policy could never emerge from the chaos of competing bureaucracies, each pursuing its own specialized interests with no agenda on a national level. Yet here, federal leadership has been tentative when it should be bold. We believe that federal officials—including the President—must promote broad strategies for basic skills improvement and academic excellence. They should insist that schools stay current with regard to computer technology, and they should encourage the often-neglected study of foreign languages. Moreover, federal officials should play a leadership role in promoting and focusing the direction of research into school effectiveness. This will require, inter alia, the upgrading of education statistics compiled by the federal government—statistics that, at present, are woefully inadequate. Likewise, the federal government should look to improve cooperation between universities and public schools on the kindergarten through twelfth-grade level. But none of this leadership requires massive federal funding if states do their job properly.

The federal government should also step into areas where there is a critical national shortage or need. For example, this country at present needs more qualified math and science teachers at the junior high and high school levels. One way in which the federal government could reasonably—and relatively inexpensively—respond to this need would be to forgive the loans of college and graduate students who matriculate in math or science and become teachers. Such a solution would have the added benefit of not being a program with a life of its own that continues on after the problem is solved.

Similarly, federal funds should be used to meet various school-related social needs. Schools that were built in the 1930s had no lunchrooms. Fifty years ago, at noon, all the students went home. Now federally funded school lunch programs are widespread, and virtually all students eat lunch in school. Once, educators never considered lunch as part of the official school day. Now, ask virtually any educator whether school includes lunch and the answer is yes.

Clearly, then, the federal government can and should mold a national policy on public education. However, it cannot effectively assume responsibility for dealing with all of the problems inherent in trying to provide a system of education. The major portion of this burden must be left to the individual states and be carried out by legislators, state boards, and state commissions of education.

The first observation to make about state regulation of public education is that it varies widely, even wildly, from state to state. Some state governments have made great strides in recent years and imposed considerable regulations and standards on local educators. New state constitutions, full-time legislatures, strong governors, reapportionment, and prodding from private citizens have combined to forge a new coalition on behalf of public education. Other states offer local school districts little in the way of guidance or support. State officials have argued at length over whether the school bell should ring eight or ten times daily, the number of holidays schools should have, and regulations concerning cancellation of classes when it snows. If they do their job properly, however, they also address three crucial policy areas.

First, state departments of education are responsible for setting minimum student competency standards as a prerequisite to promotion and receipt of a high school diploma. A diploma should stand for something—a guarantee that certain minimum standards have been attained—not just that a student has sat through two years of social studies, a year of language, and so on. Many present regulations are improperly focused, emphasizing services children have been given rather than skills they have achieved. The amount of services provided to students is important, but the true test of education is what students have learned. States must attest to the achievement of certain skills by their students. States must ensure that diplomas are real. The trend toward state-imposed minimum student competency requirements has accelerated in recent years, and these requirements should become law in all fifty states. This move, however, must be directed toward improving the performance of students. Competency tests should not be viewed as a mechanism for punishing schools or students who fail. They must be nondiscriminatory and coordinated with a curriculum that students have been given time and the proper instruction to learn.

Second, state governments have the power to set standards for teachers and other professionals within the public school system. Unfortunately, this obligation is too seldom met. Many school districts are doomed from the start because they hire and retain people who are not capable educators. Entry-level qualifications are often vague and ambiguous or too easy to obtain. Too often, state departments of education approve the credentials of all graduates of teachers colleges within the state. It is imperative that professional standards be upgraded and set firmly in place in every state. Moreover, they cannot be standards defined by the higher educational community alone; nor can they be standards expressed solely in terms of "three years of study in this area and two years of that." They must ensure that subject matter content has been mastered—particularly with regard to those teaching specific subjects on the high school level, where what a teacher knows is often more important than how well he or she knows how to teach it. In sum, serious testing of teacher candidates—with some applicants not making the grade—is essential in upgrading teacher staffs. The value of the standard should not be equated strictly with the percentage of candidates passing, but some failure will be necessary to ensure the value of success. And the standards for professionals coming into the system must be maintained throughout the system and throughout an individual's term of employment. If an educator does not perform properly—be it a teacher, administrator, or other professional—that person should be removed from the job.

Finally, state governments have considerable power with regard to school financing, and with that power comes the responsibility to make sure that no region of the state is disadvantaged because it is a poor rural or urban area whose residents vote infrequently or have less political and economic clout than their neighbors. The tendency to discriminate in the financing of public education is nationwide, and state officials have an obligation to demonstrate leadership in this area. Here, as elsewhere, the principle is justice. Rich parts of a state and poor parts of a state are not equal in terms of their ability to finance education. And, without reform, the already wide gap between "rich schools" and "poor schools" will grow wider. Moreover, if state officials fail to address the issue of equity in financing, court cases challenging tax levies and the division of funds are inevitable. Ultimately, such lawsuits will diminish the ability of these same officials to direct and control their own school systems within the state. Also with regard to equitable financing, state governors must play a far greater role than they have so far. It's not enough for a state's chief executive to ask Washington, D.C., for more money. The task of educating children has traditionally been—and will remain—primarily a state and local matter. The office of the governor in every state should be used to promote equity in education, a consideration too often left to the legislative process, where it is poorly handled.

Clearly, then, federal and state officials have a compelling responsibility and a crucial role to play in public education. They cannot, however, lose sight of the fact that, in the end, many decisions made on behalf of children are best made in the presence of children—looking a student in the eye. This means that government officials must abstain from legislating and directing in areas where it is inappropriate for them to act. They must resist the natural tendency on the part of those in power to overreach. They must avoid moving decisions that belong in classrooms to a place far away from the local level—a federal bureaucracy or some distant corner of the state. If this tendency can be curbed, and if federal and state officials exercise their power in an appropriately restrained manner, public education will be more likely to prosper and educators will feel that they are being more fully supported in their service to children.

The Judiciary

The entry of the judiciary into public education stems largely from the failure of the political process. There is a notion among some public officials that legislators should be free to pass statutes without giving serious consideration to their constitutionality and that the executive branch of government can ignore legitimate grievances until the courts tell them otherwise. This has led to increased judicial involvement with regard to public schools, both on a philosophical and an operational level. We believe that it is the responsibility of every public official to uphold the law in affirmative fashion. The job of law enforcement should not be left solely to the courts. Indeed, judges should substitute their views for those of educators as seldom as possible. However, in several areas of education policy, the role of the judiciary has been paramount.

No review of public education would be complete without mention of *Brown* v. *Board of Education* and its progeny. Quite possibly, there will never be an act by any branch of government that does more to reaffirm our ideals as a nation than the 1954 Supreme Court decision that outlawed formal segregation in the public schools. But even while recognizing this and other contributions made by the judiciary to public education, one must nonetheless question several instances where courts have actively intervened in the day-to-day affairs of school districts to the detriment of those students the schools serve.

The judiciary is obligated to define broad responsibilities and hold school districts accountable for failure to meet those standards. We do not, however, feel it appropriate for courts to assume the role of superadministrator. Cases involving matters of "special education" for handicapped children serve as a dramatic example in point.

Historically, youngsters with handicapping conditions were unwelcome in public schools and excluded from participating in programs with "ordinary" students. Some jurisdictions instituted special schools for the deaf and blind, but, generally, there was no legal obligation to educate the handicapped in public schools. Indeed, in some places, handicapped students were barred entirely from school programs. All this changed radically in 1975 when Congress passed the Education for All Handicapped Children Act, which became effective in October 1977. This law required that (1) all children with handicapping conditions be identified, evaluated, and provided with a free and appropriate education; (2) children with handicapping conditions participate in regular educational programs to the maximum extent possible; (3) nondiscriminatory procedures be used to evaluate and place children, with parents participating in the decision-making process; (4) an individualized educational program be developed for each child with handicapping conditions, to be reviewed and revised annually; and (5) handicapped children be placed in private schools at no cost to parents when an appropriate educational program is unavailable in the public school system.

The underlying goal of the federal statute was laudable. It was designed to redress a legitimate grievance and place handicapped children in an environment where their handicaps would restrict them as little as possible. In practice, however, the act has thrown school systems across the country into turmoil.

Congress enacted the law and promised to fund additional expenditures occasioned by the entitlements, but has so far failed to do so. Then the Department of Health, Education and Welfare promulgated federal regulations requiring "timely" evaluation and placement. After that, state education departments added regulations of their own, sometimes interpreting the federal guidelines as requiring evaluation and placement of all students found in need of special education within sixty days. No sooner was the ink dry on the paper than federal courts were entertaining class-action lawsuits mandating a host of services. These lawsuits—and the resulting activist judicial involvement—have tied the hands of educators and made it impossible for them to do much of what they think is right for children. School officials have been forced to act as creatures of the courts, following convoluted rules they don't believe in and, in some instances, don't understand. Parents of "special ed" children find themselves in conflict with parents of "mainstream" children over school budgets and program issues. The courts have validated and virtually locked in cement a "reform" that has never been fully tested or fully developed by any educator. A whole set of entitlements has been put in place without anyone really defining what special education is supposed to accomplish for the handicapped child.

Special education is now regarded as the bane of virtually every school administrator in the country. By federal mandate, school districts were, until recently, charged with classifying 12 percent of their students as "handicapped" in the manner of an affirmative action quota. In Boston, almost 20 percent of all public school students are in special education classes. Other large cities are in comparable situations. Often, youngsters who are deaf and blind are categorized with students who are constantly in trouble in school and therefore labeled "emotionally handicapped." A disproportionately high percentage of these "emotionally handicapped" students are black and Hispanic, whereas a disproportionate number of white children are found in special categories that call for tutorial services, thereby raising an entire new set of questions regarding discriminatory practice.

Nothing that has happened in the past thirty years has done more to drive the cost of education up than implementation of the Education for All Handicapped Children Act. It is a statute that exemplifies entitlements run amok. Three times as much money is spent per capita on special education students as on other youngsters, much of it wastefully spent. In New York, for example, all special education students are provided with door-to-door bus transportation in accordance with State Department of Education regulations. The New York City Council has added to that by insisting that a matron travel on each bus. Insofar as the matron is concerned, politics controls the logic of the entitlement. The city receives 90 percent reimbursement for transportation costs from the state, and the matrons belong to a politically powerful union—hence their jobs. The morass of regulations is so outlandish that brothers and sisters attending the same school can be required to travel on separate buses because one is "handicapped" and the other is not. Money spent in the best interests of special education youngsters would not be spent in this manner.

Many educators still believe that public schools should steer clear of educating the handicapped. We disagree. But the problem with special education programs as presently constituted is that, sound judgment to the contrary, the courts have mandated certain services for children—services immune by court decree from current fiscal restraints—without focusing on results. Handicapped students' entitlements are defined by their condition—not by whether their needs are being met. There is nothing in the court orders to ensure that handicapped children are being well educated—only that X services are being provided and Y number of dollars are being spent. It is as though the Environmental Protection Agency decided to base automobile emission standards on the amount of money spent for pollution-control devices rather than the quantity and quality of emission exhaust. And the result of this folly has been to condemn large numbers of children to classes where there is an artificial regulatory and judicially encouraged limit to what is expected of them— because they have been classified as handicapped. Regular modes of academic assessment are precluded because, if schools were to assess these students as they do "normal" children, they would be guilty of "discrimination." There is little discipline, because a school that holds a special education youngster to its code of student conduct is "depriving him of his entitlements." In essence, the elements of good schooling are not practiced. Instead of learning what he or she *can* do and how to do it, special education youngsters get individual educational programs that relegate them to inferior classes and excuse them from performing to the same standards as their peers. They are told that they are not equal to other children; the ultimate responsibility of the system to turn them into producers is diminished; and the children themselves are doomed to lifetimes of lower expectations. They are spared the sometimes frustrating classroom experience of being unable to do but, at the same time, are condemned to the certainty of doing less. And, in the face of all this, there has been virtual silence from the commentators of school reform.

Typical of this situation was the fate of an experimental high school program conducted by the City of New York. Its aim was to bring handicapped children and regular students together in one class on the theory that, if special education youngsters were "mainstreamed," it would improve their performance. The program was invalidated because it did not segregate resources in a way that accountants monitoring special education expenditures could follow. The accountants demanded separate, discrete services—hence different teachers for regular and handicapped students. Those with final authority were not looking at which program would better meet the needs of children. They didn't look at which program produced better results. Instead, they viewed the mainstream program with distrust—distrust for how honestly the school system was dealing with the handicapped. The regulations originally designed to help handicapped children were distorted to the point where they were seen as necessary to protect handicapped children from their own school system. The city's schools were told, "We give you the children; we trust you to teach them; but we don't trust you to determine the manner in which they should be taught. And we refuse to look at the end result—which program does a better job of educating the handicapped."

Obviously, there are many instances where special education services have provided real benefits to genuinely handicapped children. But few people who have worked closely with students believe that upward of 10 percent of them are so handicapped as to need the clinical services, instructional isolation, and lower expectations characteristic of today's special education programs. The way in which these programs have grown out of control underscores the fact that educational entitlements must be based on the practice of good schooling—not on individual rights as mandated by the judiciary. Federal judges have to realize that, as regards the day-to-day administrative functioning of local school districts, judicial intervention is largely unwarranted.

Local School Districts and School Boards

No blueprint for education, however admirable, can be effective without proper implementation at the local level. Yet, all too often, local school districts are more concerned with political influence than education and fail to provide a framework that enables schools to prosper.

The first thing to be said about America's local school districts is that there are too many of them—roughly sixteen thousand in all. In theory, a multiplicity of school districts enables each community to adapt its schools to meet local needs and preferences. In reality, it results in poor standards and inadequate instruction.

School districts provide the legal and institutional framework within which individual schools operate. Some localization is desirable, but America doesn't need sixteen thousand separate entities to do the job. Notwithstanding the fact that our public schools are locally directed—unlike those in France, Germany, and Israel, where there is national control—variation in educational programs is simply not great enough to justify so many separate units. A visitor who walks into one school in Oregon, another in Maine, and a third in Nebraska will see uniform nine-to-three instruction with summers off and the same basic curriculum in each. Too many school districts leads to poor administration and deprives students of the economies of scale. You simply cannot expect a school district with just one high school to provide the unique services that fill the needs of all children. Enriched programs and alternative programs require a budget capability and variation in personnel that small districts cannot offer, and there are too many obstacles to make sharing resources among districts a feasible alternative. Thus, political prerogatives that lead to the creation of small school districts must be surrendered for the good of children. And, although there is no "ideal" size for a school district, those educators who look seriously at school reform must question whether their districts are large enough to provide adequate opportunities for children—particularly for high school students, who require a greater variety of programs.

We believe that America's school districts should be realigned—continuing a process of consolidation that has already begun—to reduce the number of small school districts and put into effect the economies of scale. We also believe that, in this process, it would be desirable to create school districts with a better ethnic mix than presently exists. Moreover, we propose that each student who attends public school be allowed to choose the school that he or she attends. That is, students should be zoned for two or more schools—five or more in urban areas—and parents should decide which of these schools is more desirable. Although this is increasingly the case with high schools—and, in some cities, intermediate schools—it is important that these options be available to the parents of elementary school children as well. The benefits in such a plan would be threefold.

First, the task of engaging students who are required to attend a particular school is more difficult than encouraging students who are there by choice. Students who come to a particular school voluntarily are more likely to be motivated, to feel good about what's happening, and to find an educational program suited to their needs. It is easier to engender enthusiasm for school when students have chosen to be there.

Second, the creation of options will allow school administrators to curtail comprehensive and often costly program offerings and concentrate on specific areas of academic interest. Schools will be able to specialize in science, the humanities, art, or language without the problem of shortchanging students who have to be there but have other academic interests.

Third, the creation of public school options will decrease the flight of students to private schools. We have little sympathy for white parents who take their children out of public schools simply because they don't want them mixing with children of another color. However, there are some valid reasons for sending a youngster to private school, including the fact that in some instances the education is better. Parents do not have an obligation to take less by sending their children to public school. Rather, it is the responsibility of a public school system to provide more—a better system—so that parents will not choose to enroll their children in a private institution. When parents—and particularly urban parents of elementary school youngsters—review their options, they often find a choice between *one* public school and dozens of private ones. Zoning for more than one school would redefine those options. It would also create competition of a positive nature between individual public schools. We have to promote some comparisons between schools and allow market forces into play. As a consequence of the competitive process engendered by multiple-school zoning, some public schools—the better ones—would prosper. Others would be faced with two choices—improve, or cease to operate. It would be quite refreshing and healthy for public schools in America to grow in enrollment or close their doors, not because of changes in population, but based on the choice of parents regarding the quality of education that various public schools offer.

Once school districts are set in place, the question then becomes, "How should they be governed?" Educators have a responsibility to put the right people in charge of schools, but too often in America today the right people are not in charge of education.

Particularly in our large cities, public schools seem to have become fair game for the advancement of political careers, graft, and corruption. School boards are often dominated by vested interests—labor unions in some cities, political idealogues or political party organizations in others. Some board members see their job as the distribution of patronage. Others use their positions as launching pads for higher elective office, capitalizing on emotional issues such as prayer in the schools and busing. There is no guarantee that public funds will be well spent. School buildings that should have been closed years ago are kept open for reasons that have nothing to do with educating children. Overbuilt administrative systems carry on because they provide jobs to the providers. The educational system is ripped off. Despite the fact that many school board members are able citizens of good character, too often school systems are regarded as dumping grounds for political hacks, a place where politicians hide their dirty laundry.

Poor-quality school boards magnify the problems faced by day-to-day school administrators. It's far more difficult to run a school system today than forty years ago. Four decades ago, values were pretty much in place, the methodology of education was time-honored, and dropouts from school "dropped in" to industrial jobs. Teachers had the luxury of dealing with students similar to those from a generation earlier. Suburbanization had just begun, and the nations' cities were prospering. Nothing had happened to focus dissatisfaction on curriculum subject matter. Sputnik was in the future; there were plenty of jobs.

It's a different world now, and local school boards—which bear the primary burden for establishing local school policy—warrant close attention. Their job is important and, if public education is to flourish in America, it must be placed in the hands of men and women who demonstrate a commitment to education. School board members should be people who read books; they should know literature, the arts, and science; they should be productive members of the community; they should be leaders.

We believe that school board members should be appointed—not elected—by the highest political authority in the area served. There should be staggered rotation, so the board is not completely responsive to the climate of

any particular moment or comprised entirely of inexperienced members beginning their task at the same time. We
favor a screening process that involves all segments of the
community. In the main, the board members ultimately
chosen should be people whose children are in public
school. Not every member need be a public school parent,
but people whose children are on the receiving end of the
decisions they're making tend to be more sober regarding
the outcome. Admittedly, the selection process we advocate will retain a measure of politics; but the world is
political. At the very least, a broad-based screening committee would eliminate well-financed candidates running
in single-issue-oriented elections, pandering to a constituency that can't see beyond an emotional social issue. Also,
a screening committee, through interviews and investiga-
tion, would be likely to determine qualifications beyond
whether or not a potential board member satisfies a particular personal relationship or political friendship.

School boards should not be dominated by professional
educators. They should be comprised of people who will
question—and, where necessary, challenge—the education establishment. Board members must never forget
that they represent *all* of the children in their district. Too
often, members chosen because they are of a particular
ethnic origin or because they live within a given geo-
graphic boundary consider themselves representatives of
that constituency alone. Yet representing less than all of
the children is representing not enough of them. Board
meetings should be held in public, except for those rare
instances when a genuine reason for secrecy exists. And,
at these meetings, real discussion and deliberation should
occur. The temptation to act in secrecy and then put on a

pro forma public show must be curbed. Also, school board members should not be paid. Allowances to board members reinforce the image of the job as a patronage plum and, in some instances, have risen to ludicrously high proportions. In New York City, for example, board members are paid on a per diem basis and have made as much as $40,000 per member per year. The job should be a giving one—not a taking one.

Once policy decisions have been made, it then becomes the job of the school superintendent, as chief executive officer of the school district, to implement them—without board interference. Too often, effective administration is stymied by board members who become overly involved in the day-to-day running of schools. When this occurs, the superintendent is reduced to puppet status and quality leadership is squandered. As with federal and state officials, one of the most important lessons that school board members can learn is when power should not be used.

School Administrators

We have said that school boards should consist of the very best people capable of overseeing schools; people whose self-interest does not derive from being in the schools; people whose interest in schools is that of a citizen concerned for the welfare of children. These people, in turn, choose the person who runs the district—the superintendent of schools.

The day-to-day mechanics of running a school system can be overwhelming. School administrators must weigh the competing interests of students, parents, teachers, cafeteria workers, and custodians. In addition to standard programs, they must provide vocational education, bilingual education, and education for the handicapped. They administer drug programs; lobby for federal, state, and local financial aid; supervise capital construction and litigation; and sometimes negotiate union contracts. The magnitude of these tasks is staggering. And beyond the matter of administrative style and individual ability, school superintendents must deal with systems so large as to almost defy management. In New York City, for example, the school bus system is larger than the entire public transportation system of Los Angeles or Chicago. The Board of Education is the largest commercial landlord in New York, responsible for the operation and maintenance of over one thousand buildings. More children are fed in New York City's school cafeterias each day than people are fed in Howard Johnson's restaurants nationwide.

The job of superintendent of schools is both administrative and political. It does not require classroom teaching expertise, although, as chief school officer, the superintendent should have both knowledge and a philosophy regarding what teaching and learning are about. Equally essential, however, is a gift for organization, an understanding of management, and mastery of the relationship between law, public administration, and education. If a superintendent of schools is not proficient in these areas, he or she will not be able to do the job well. And if the superintendent's job is poorly done, no amount of public relations gimmickry will save the schools from the brunt of that incompetence.

Superintendents are constrained in the exercise of power by a host of factors, including the usual bureaucratic limitations on the capacity to be creative. Staff changes must be carried out in accord with elaborate civil service regulations and collective bargaining agreements. Budgetary considerations include limited funds and restrictions on the allocation of resources so that, often, a surplus in one area cannot be used to offset deficits in another. Superintendents must know "the system" and how to deal with it. This is a task that cannot be delegated. Yet, in too many instances, superintendents receive less than adequate support from school boards and local political leaders. Often, they are replaced before fledgling programs have a chance to develop. In large cities, the average tenure of a superintendent of schools is less than three years—testimony to the perils of the job.

The qualities that make a good superintendent are similar to those required of any able chief executive officer. And, as with any well-run business, a superintendent's choice of appointees is critical. The most crucial of these appointees are principals—the men and women who manage the district's schools.

No single individual in a given school is as important as the principal. Like school superintendents, principals are administrators and managers of often limited resources. They must coordinate the demands of teachers, students, parents, and district-office administrators. They are like the center of a wheel whose spokes keep changing. They must be strong leaders who set the tone and standards for their schools. And given today's educational climate— where the acquisition of basic skills is greatly dependent on which school a student attends—the role of principal becomes even more crucial. School principals are the instructional leaders of their schools. They must constantly visit classes, observe teachers, and evaluate their performance. In schools that are improving, it is almost always the case that the principal is an assertive leader and disciplinarian who has assumed full responsibility for the fulfillment of standards and achievement of basic goals. Yet standards for the selection and training of principals and evaluation of their own performance seldom exist. And, when they do, such standards are often quite arbitrary and peculiar to a given district and its politics. Indeed, studies show that, in many districts, principals are chosen for reasons not even known to the candidates themselves. By way of example, in New York City, for decades, principals were selected on the basis of a licensing examination that tested what candidates knew about educational philosophy but bore no relationship to how well they had performed as teachers or administrators in school. The test makers simply refused to evaluate the relationship between test results and the prior work of candidates for the job of principal. Thus, unsatisfactory employees were often licensed for promotion to principal by the same school system in which they had failed as teachers. It was the equivalent of the Los Angeles Raiders fielding a football team by selecting players who could pass a test on the mechanics of football rather than players who could play it. Yet not until 1970 was this procedure voided by the federal courts and, because of state law and union power, remnants of the old mechanism still exist. To this day, there is little attention paid to what constitutes an "effective" principal, even though the principal is key in determining what goals and directions a school will take and is the supervisor of day-to-day activity in the school.

Principals *can* make a difference, more so perhaps than

any other local educator. It is essential that they exercise power conscientiously, wisely, and with skill. Good things do not happen by accident in public schools. School districts must select their principals with care, encourage and support them, and develop standards to hold them accountable for their success or failure as educators.

Teachers and Their Unions

To some, teaching looks easy. It is not. It is one of the most challenging jobs in society and a very difficult thing to do.

Good teaching is not just a gift of nature. It is an acquired skill that needs to be refined constantly. The best teachers have intelligence, patience, dedication, and the ability to communicate discipline, basic skills, and high moral values. Also, they like children. A basic ingredient of teaching is the feeling that students are good people to spend time with, that they can learn, and that teachers are critical to success of the learning process.

There has been a lot of discussion lately about the quality of teachers in America's public school system. The consensus is that starting teachers are not as good as they used to be and that, despite the presence of many first-rate new teachers, the pool of available candidates has been dramatically reduced. Teachers themselves know that society values their efforts less than in years gone by. In 1969, 75 percent of Americans polled said they would like a child of theirs to take up a career teaching in the public schools. In 1983, that figure was down to 45 percent. Yet even as society accords teachers less respect, it gives them more to do. The job of teaching is more demanding and difficult today than ever, because children are coming to school with greater needs and far less preparation than they had before.

People who want to be teachers are generally driven by respect for learning and a love of children. They like books, feel comfortable in a classroom setting, and are interested in guiding students toward adulthood. Yet, increasingly, teachers find themselves preoccupied by the siege mentality that has developed in our public schools. Often, they have no role in formulating the instructional strategy and design of classes. Unhappiness builds as they come to believe that their ability to help children has been impaired and that excessive power is concentrated in the hands of school administrators.

Community pressures, such as the drive for minority hiring in urban areas, further exacerbate these tensions. America's teachers are largely white. They reflect what the student population was thirty years ago. This is the way of public education. In our cities, when a majority of students were ethnic whites, the teachers were largely Anglo-Saxon Protestants. Now the teachers are ethnic whites; the students are black and Hispanic. There is a real benefit in the strong presence of minority teachers in public schools—particularly in areas where schoolchildren are largely minority. However, there is no way that minority teachers can be represented in schools today in proportion to the number of minority students. There are simply not enough trained professionals in the minority community willing to enter the teaching profession. In twenty years—when the present generation of students grows to adulthood—there will be. But to expect instant racial parity is unrealistic—and minority hiring at any cost, when it leads to the hiring of unqualified teachers, is a disservice to *all* students.

Compared with other civil servants—police officers, sanitation workers, motor vehicle bureau employees— teachers hold their own well. Given the manner in which education has been shortchanged lately, teachers show more care and compassion than the public might expect. But there are ways in which teachers have underevaluated themselves and their capacity for positive change. Limited by "the system" and beset by the loss of a professional image in the face of their own union stridency, they have often allowed their growth as teachers to be stifled. These shortcomings must be addressed if students are to be well served by schools.

One criticism justifiably leveled at some public school teachers is that they tend to see teaching as a closed art. When a teacher goes into the classroom for the first time, it is after a minimum of sixteen years of watching other people teach. It's very hard to change preconceptions about the goals and structure of classroom learning after that kind of exposure. Unlike doctors or lawyers, whose first months in professional school are spent with professors who disabuse them of notions acquired in high school and college, beginning teachers think they know their roles well. They see approval in conformity that shies away from creativity and innovation—a view reinforced by prevailing teacher education courses.

Moreover, in recent years, teachers have come to rely upon the union contract as the standard for professional responsibility. The rights of teachers in most school districts are secured by collective bargaining. However, instead of defining the minimum performance that is expected of a teacher, these agreements have come to be regarded as the standard by which teachers are supposed to act. A teacher is obligated by contract to be in class by a given hour, and this is translated by some into a right. Instead of saying, "I must be there by eight-thirty," the teacher interprets his or her obligation as "I shouldn't get there until eight-thirty." Soon, teachers begin to think that the contract represents the whole of their professional obligations and they refuse to do anything not required by the contract.

It is impossible—and it would be wrong—to embody every single responsibility a teacher has to students in a union contract. Contracts represent an entitlement to the teacher. But contracts by themselves are simply not appropriate to the development of an educational community. Yet too often school principals find teachers unwilling to perform fundamental chores necessary to building a school community because those chores are not mandated by the collective bargaining agreement.

Teachers are public officials. The most important responsibility a public official has is to discharge the duties of office. When teachers refuse to do the best job they can, it hurts. When teachers maintain that they have no more duty to students than members of the United Auto Workers Union have to Ford or Chrysler, it is painful. Meanwhile, the problems surrounding collective bargaining continue to grow, as fiscal pressures mount, the demand for increased teacher productivity intensifies, and teachers union leaders brand efforts to reform contracts as attempts to "break the union's back" rather than efforts to help children.

At present, there are four areas of national concern with regard to union power, and the first of these is teacher salaries. Relative to other professionals with comparable training, those salaries are low, and some people don't go into teaching because of them.

We believe that it is the job of school administrators to secure a fair wage for teachers. School systems cannot promote justice for students and, at the same time, deny justice to teachers. However, we do not believe that compensation is or ever has been the basis for teachers coming to work. Historically, teachers have chosen their profession for other reasons, and the large number of teachers in parochial and secular private schools—where salaries are often well below public school levels—attests to this fact. Those teachers are there because they get a sense of importance and fulfillment from their work.

Even a substantial increase in teachers' salaries would not by itself make a real difference in the quality of teachers recruited by America's public schools. It would simply drive up the cost of teachers already at work. This is not to say that salary increases are unwarranted. Rather, we should not expect the quality of teachers to change much because of increased pay.

If teachers with advanced skills in math or science are needed, it would be more cost-efficient to offer those presently in the system an opportunity to obtain such skills. Find several teachers who want to know more about physics. Give them a semester's leave to enroll at a university program to learn physics on an advanced level. Teacher sabbaticals are granted by many school districts, but rarely does the district reap a benefit proportional or even related to the expense. Now is the time to make these sabbaticals more productive for the districts that pay for them.

Now is also the time to put a cap on salary increments that bear little or no relationship to school system needs or teacher performance. In many public school systems, salary differentials are given to teachers with masters degrees and other graduate credits. The rationale for this salary increment is that it will encourage teachers to develop the type of expertise needed for teacher improvement. Instead, salary differentials for graduate school credits have often turned to scandal. In New York City, for example, teachers began taking fraudulent mail-order courses. In one instance, a "golf by mail" course served as the basis for a salary differential. Did the teachers know it was a fraud? Yes, and so did the academic institutions that supplied the credits. Yet the New York City school bureaucracy authorized the courses and raised the participants' salaries. The result was that standards fell precipitously; the teachers union supported salary differentials for worthless courses already taken; and it took years for the chancellor's office to remedy the situation. It was a clear-cut example of entitlements run amok and the abuse of an agreement secured by collective bargaining.

Teacher layoffs as linked to the issue of seniority also merit examination. In recent years, declining public school enrollment and budget cuts have forced hiring freezes and, in some cases, teacher layoffs in school districts across the country. It is a cornerstone of union philosophy and most collective bargaining agreements that the last person hired is the first person out. Thus, the layoffs have resulted in a substantial increase in the average age and seniority of teachers, leaving students with instructors who are often less aware of new teaching methods and changes in subject matter. Many minority teachers who are among the "most recently hired" have been terminated, as have numerous other able young instructors.

We believe that job security based on seniority is less important than having the best teachers available for students. Judgments have to be made on the basis of what's best for children, and it is not necessarily the last teacher hired who ought to be fired first. Still, we recognize that long, dedicated service deserves consideration. One partial solution to the problem would be for teachers to be hired and categorized on the basis of subject matter expertise in intermediate and high schools. Then, if separations were necessary, they could be made on the basis of last-in in a particular area. That way, if the last five teachers hired in a school were math teachers and five layoffs were necessary, the layoffs could be apportioned among those with the least seniority in five different subject matter departments—one layoff in each. A better system—albeit one that would meet with strong union opposition—would be to terminate the weakest teacher in each subject matter area. However, such a system would require safeguards to ensure that teacher layoffs were made on the basis of ability—or lack thereof—not on the basis of which teacher had the *most* seniority and hence the highest salary the school system could erase. There are no easy answers. Letting someone go at the top to save someone else at the bottom unsettles the lives of all teachers. But some accommodation has to be reached if children are to be better served.

A third area where we would like to see reform of

teacher entitlements involves flexibility in teacher assignments. Teachers tend not to see their lesson plans wearing out. They become wedded to a particular subject and way of teaching, and even to their own homeroom, with the result that, often, creativity is lost. Administrators should be allowed greater flexibility in rotating course assignments and even school assignments for teachers. Too often, strong union contracts impose managerial limitations on school administrators so that staff members cannot be freely transferred. People are put in positions and can stay there forever. Thus, a person who becomes a teacher stays in the same school until retirement. It is very hard for school officials to come in and say, "We are going to transfer some people to another school for the good of the system." That is interpreted as punishment. But reassignment is not punishment. It can be an opportunity for rejuvenation, offering new challenges and infusing the system with new energy. Indeed, administrators should be trained in how to change assignments effectively. Also, there should be more leeway in assigning teachers to nonclassroom duties such as hall patrol and after-school work. In building a real school community, teachers must be available for a variety of chores that go beyond the academic core, and they must see these chores as their professional obligation.

In sum, we are suggesting modification of union contracts in several ways that will affect basically good teachers. There is an even greater need for reform with regard to teachers who are dishonest or inept. The job of teaching, as previously stated, is more demanding now than ever before. Yet there is no escape from the fact that teaching requires greater talent and ability than some of our teachers possess.

We believe that teachers have an absolute right to protection against being dealt with in an arbitrary or capricious manner. They must be free to teach without fear of being dismissed as a consequence of personal bias or minor policy disagreements. But this right does not justify inadequate teacher performance, which violates the entitlement of students to learn from competent teachers who merit trust and respect.

Tenure is too easily granted to teachers in public school systems. A teacher at the college level understands that earning tenure is very difficult. By contrast, teachers in public schools—grades kindergarten through twelve—*expect* that tenure will be granted. There is a presumption of entitlement before the event, fueled in part by the fact that standards for hiring teachers are often too low to begin with and sustained by the failure to have meaningful review of teacher performance. The granting of tenure should not be automatic—nor should it be permanent.

Beyond that, not enough is being done to improve the performance of teachers who have passed probation and received tenure. In the case of inept teachers, the problem is particularly acute, and often it is not that the teacher got worse. Rather, it is that a poor teacher was tenured in the first place. When this occurs, a school system's first obligation is to make every effort to help that teacher. You can't run a school system that says all students can learn and then deny that same opportunity to teachers. However, once all efforts for sufficient improvement have been exhausted, if the teacher is still not capable of performing properly, the system has a clear obligation to remove that teacher. And very often, because of collective bargaining rights and state legislation obtained as a consequence of union pressure, this task is next to impossible to accomplish. Reform is urgently needed here—particularly in union-dominated states—and it will take courage because, invariably, removal of an inept teacher is a procedure that teachers unions fight vigorously without regard to the welfare of children who must suffer through that teacher's classes.

The problem is further magnified in instances where teachers have acted immorally or in violation of law. On December 6, 1978, a New York City public school teacher was convicted of a felony for smuggling forty thousand pounds of marijuana into the United States. Upon conviction, the teacher was suspended *with pay*. On January 3, 1979, probable cause was found for the teacher's removal. The hearing date was set for four and a half months later, on May 13, 1979. The teacher's brief was submitted two months after that, and a trial was held on October 23, 1979. On February 7, 1980, the decision was finally made to suspend the teacher without pay pending resolution of the appeal on his criminal conviction. It took the system well over a year from the time of conviction for a major felony to get that teacher off the public payroll, and all that time he was getting paid the same salary as teachers who were setting a good example for their students and doing their job properly.

Disciplinary proceedings have to move more quickly than they do at present in order to eliminate teachers who are not doing their job. There are too many ways that professionals who are inattentive to the needs of children continue to maintain their position in America's public school system. In some states, teachers suspended with cause have gone through three or four years in the courts before a final confirmation of wrongdoing—and during that period, the teacher accumulates three or four more years of pension credit in addition to salary.

Public education is improperly served by a "due process" system so time-consuming and complex that it shields dishonesty and incompetence. The result of such a system is that good teachers are demoralized and children suffer. There is no justice in having an inept or criminal teacher on the public payroll. Those few teachers must be eliminated, and the tragedy of the present system is that it takes far too long to accomplish that end. It does not advance the cause of good teaching or good teachers to have rules and regulations that contradict what public education is all about. Yet this is precisely what we have today because, in the process of unionization, teacher organizers have too often organized against school management. We hope that, as teachers unions grow more secure, this militancy abates.

Teaching is a noble profession. Teachers are role models for our children. Wisely exercised, the power of teachers can restore our schools to their former position of high honor and respect. But much had to be done to reshape the role and responsibilities of our teachers.

Other Special Interest Groups

The political power of miscellaneous special interest groups varies from state to state and even within each school district. This further fragments educational policy and reform. Money is needed for many programs, but, particularly where discretion is involved, it tends to be spent where political influence is greatest or in response to those who demand the loudest. Decisions regarding which schools should be opened or closed in a given neighborhood often turn not on the basis of where it is convenient for children to travel, but on which neighborhood is better connected politically. Lucrative transportation contracts are awarded to school bus companies without true competitive bidding or regard for past on-time and safety records.

It is very difficult sometimes to get people to make educational decisions on behalf of children. It's hard for politicians and educators to say no to certain people, and we understand that. But the men and women who direct America's public school system have to remember that they are supposed to be leading that system somewhere—and many vested interests will have to be disappointed for the sake of a broader agenda on behalf of children. This point might seem simple and very basic, but educators must be constantly reminded of it. Their obligation to children must remain paramount.

Vested interests and special interest groups are not all bad or misguided. It hurts to eliminate some of their programs from the system, but this is an era of hard choices. The challenge to deliver a first-rate educational product with efficiency and economy demands that special interests be curbed. Yet the history of educators refusing to say no and thereby adding unnecessary costs to the educational process is a long one.

The use of paraprofessionals as teacher assistants in urban classrooms is a case in point. The paraprofessional movement sprang less from educational design than from a strategy for giving jobs to people who were unemployed in city job markets during the 1960s. The great majority were minority women with a high school diploma as their only educational qualification. Without federal funding and a crisis in the nation's cities, it's unlikely that the paraprofessional movement would have started, let alone grown. Most educators agree that there are other, more effective ways to spend federal funds on behalf of children. Yet, in many cities today, paraprofessionals are a powerful special interest lobby.

We don't think a classroom teacher needs a paraprofessional to teach properly. Children would be better served by smaller classes with greater personal contact between teacher and student. If a school system has extra money, it should be used to reduce class size and hire more teachers to strengthen the student-teacher bond— particularly for the early grades. Schools can hire three teachers for approximately the same price as two teachers and two paraprofessionals. It makes far more sense to have three teachers teaching twenty students each, than two teachers coupled with two paraprofessionals in two classes of thirty.

Far more sensitive and complex than the use of paraprofessionals are the issues that surround bilingual education—another special interest project. Bilingual education springs from a need and a desire. The need is that of many children who have the entitlement to a public school education and speak only a native language other than English—most often, Spanish. The desire is that of advocates for these children, who ask that they retain their cultural heritage to the greatest extent possible. In both instances, bilingual education assists children in finding their identity in the school system and works to teach them subject matter. However, in recent years, bilingual education has become as much a political issue as an educational one, with school administrators often standing back and watching politicians become experts in the field of education. And the matter of bilingual education—its content and its very existence—has become a subject of considerable controversy.

Much of the anti-bilingual-education dogma is fueled by people who aren't particularly sympathetic toward Hispanics. Their arguments, when grounded on prejudice and bias, are best discarded. However, two legitimate grievances with regard to bilingual education do exist. First, in many school districts, there simply aren't enough qualified teachers and supervisors available to do an adequate job of educating foreign-language-speaking children. As a result, many youngsters in bilingual programs are growing up educationally deficient both in English *and* their native language. This problem is compounded by the fact that, often, bilingual teachers are poorly supervised and programs for evaluating the effectiveness of instruction are poorly developed. Indeed, it is frequently unclear whether a particular bilingual program has been designed to maintain foreign customs or speed a child's transition to English-language competence.

Also, and equally important, bilingual education runs counter to the spirit and meaning of *Brown* v. *Board of Education*. The logic of that decision by the United States Supreme Court was that separate is inherently unequal; a society that seeks to isolate one class of citizens on the basis of race is disadvantaging those children and weakening all of society. The dominant characteristic of bilingual education programs as presently practiced is a class of children—most often, Hispanic—sitting in one classroom while the bulk of the student population learns its lessons in another. The longer this situation continues, the less equal the students who are isolated become.

It is our view that the first priority of all education programs for foreign-language-speaking students should be the development of English-language proficiency as quickly as possible. We realize the tremendous challenge that the children of immigrants face in coming to a strange land, leaving all that is familiar behind, and having to acquire a new language. However, we would do these children a great injustice if our goals were any less. Literacy in English is essential for children to enter the mainstream of American society and excel in our English-dominant culture. Having said this, however, we add that schools cannot wait until a child is fully competent in English to begin instruction in other areas. Therefore, insofar as feasible, we should teach all subjects to children in a language they can understand. And since knowledge of a second language is a great asset, we would encourage foreign-language-speaking children to maintain proficiency in their native language at the same time they are enrolled in language transition programs.

In no instance should transition programs extend beyond a maximum of three years. At the end of three years, properly taught, these children should be able to perform in English. If not, they should be held back in school until a sufficient level of English competency has been reached for them to be responsive in English-speaking classes. In this regard, we add that our forebears, in the main, handled the transition to English quite well. The past success of our public schools in assimiliating immigrant children has been so notable, particularly when compared to the assimilation of immigrants in other countries, that a similar prescription makes sense in today's schools. Children who are expected to perform will perform. Children who are told they must learn English will learn English—if adequately taught.

The Business Community

Good government and what's good for business do not always coincide, but, clearly, it is vital to business that our public school system do a better job. This is not to say that public schools should train students to assure particular types of employment. But today's economy requires workers who have sounder academic preparation and a higher level of education than ever before. Yet, in the face of this need, we find a shortage of workers with critical skills and a dwindling pool of qualified high school graduates to choose from.

In the nineteenth century, before compulsory education, business leaders promoted schooling among our citizens. Then, when compulsory education became a reality, the business community was prominently represented on local school boards Business leaders—large and small—understood the need for building a nation, and they were involved in education. They fought for public schools and offered support for expanded educational programs. Their influence upon the body politic was strong, and school construction became a symbol of what they did well. Buildings constructed under their influence were imposing and proud. In New York City, Jamaica High School sits on top of a commanding hill in Queens, as does Curtis High School on Staten Island. At Manhattan's highest point, George Washington High overlooks New Jersey, the Hudson River, and the Bronx. Benjamin Franklin High School and Fort Hamilton High School are magnificent structures, typical of their era, hailed by architectural critics even today. Schools built fifty years ago looked out over the city and demanded that the populace notice them. It's obvious they meant something to the community when they were built.

American business today has an even greater self-interest in public education than in the past. Our economy needs entry level workers who have mastered basic skills at a far higher level than before. Yet, over the past several decades, much of the business community has walked away from its responsibility to public schools. This trend accelerated in the 1960s, when school involvement became a "risky business," with demonstrators protesting and picketing outside board members' homes. Simultaneously, the nature of business leadership became more transitory. Corporations began buying and selling one another with greater frequency. Small local businesses were bought by large conglomerates. Business leaders became absorbed with maintaining their own jobs. The growth of suburbs also had an impact on the contribution of the business community to urban schools. People of influence no longer worked in the same community where they lived. Particularly in urban areas, they no longer had as great a personal stake in the end product of public schools. The changing composition of student bodies—the presence of many minority students in school —also led to a definite, if difficult to measure, reduction in enthusiasm and support from the business community for public education. To many business leaders, the children of America's cities were no longer their own.

High schools are no longer built the way they used to be. The decline of America's public schools is evident even in physical terms. Often, schools are hidden in out-of-the-way places and on narrow streets. They look like factories. Children no longer travel past the offices and homes of influential businessmen to get to school.

American business still has enormous power to influence public education, as evidenced by the imposition of competency testing as a diploma prerequisite in more than forty states nationwide. That movement was spearheaded by business leaders appalled at the lack of skills acquired by students. Now, what is needed is a formula and a commitment that will enable us to regain the full support that business once gave to American education.

Probably the most significant contribution the business community can make to education relates to jobs. It is very rare for school officials to successfully promote work experience. Most teachers and school administrators are largely unfamiliar with job markets and unable to give students an informed judgment about "the world out there." The link between schools and jobs must be more clearly established, with the ultimate goal being that a high school diploma guarantees a job—not a "make-work job," but a job that has been earned by the applicant's skill and work competency.

Schooling, if well done, leads to a job. This is the idea

that policy makers should aim for. And to achieve this goal, American business leaders can and must help educators develop programs that will ensure that students coming out of school are capable of performing as tomorrow's jobs will require them to perform. We advocate linkage between schools and the business community to establish the following: (1) part-time jobs for students while school is in session; (2) summer employment; and (3) the development of programs that will prepare students for full-time work after graduation, with an accent on local businesses actually providing jobs.

Ideally, every student should be required to hold a job, paid or volunteer, for some period of time as a condition of earning a high school diploma. This experience would teach youngsters the rules of the workplace and the value of employment. But, to succeed in this era of intolerable youth unemployment, such a program will depend on the retraining of teacher staffs and the business community providing jobs.

American business can also contribute substantially to public education through "join-a-school" programs that link corporations to a particular school. Join-a-school projects already exist in many areas of the country and take many forms. For example, IBM donates computer equipment, supplies expertise in developing programs for students, operates a computer job fair, and takes other practical steps to help students achieve long-range goals. In New York City, Manufacturer's Hanover Trust Company offers a different type of support, focusing its efforts on extracurricular activities that build school spirit and a sense of community. American Can Company held its annual shareholders meeting in May 1984 in New York at its joined-with school—Martin Luther King Jr. High School. In Philadelphia, Atlanta, Oakland, Chicago, Indianapolis, Los Angeles, and Washington, D.C., substantial join-a-school programs have been developed. CBS has "joined" schools in each city in which it has a wholly owned local television station. In some of these programs, youngsters attend meetings with businesspeople, staff-training sessions are sponsored, and job guarantees are given to students who pursue a particular course of study. In others, modern technology is introduced to the schools —replacing manual typewriters with word-processing systems for students and administrative staff—and traditional courses in vocational education have been revitalized by introducing students to the operation of heavy industry trades.

If every public school in the country could be matched with a corporation interested in its development, public education would be substantially enhanced. Students would have more of a sense that their needs were being filled. Teachers and administrators would feel less alone. The results of join-a-school projects to date have been positive. We need more of them. If America's businessmen and businesswomen were willing to go into schools en masse and say, "We want to help; tell us your problems; we will put people and resources at your disposal," the benefits would be enormous. And these programs need not be limited to "big business." Labor unions, private human services agencies, small businesses, and other entities can offer support. The key to a successful join-a-school program is the time, effort, and personal commitment of a company's workers—not a contribution measured in dollars.

Public schools would also gain from lateral entry into the ranks of the teaching profession. More and more often in American society, people are opting for careers that are temporary in nature. Men and women no longer typically spend forty years with the same company. Instead, they move from industry to industry and job to job, carrying a multitude of skills with them. At present, school district administrators face a situation where some of their best staff members succumb to the lure of private industry. The corollary to this is that many gifted people in private industry could be enticed away from their jobs into teaching. Certainly, a number of successful college programs are staffed by professors who have left earlier careers in favor of academia. The same phenomenon could occur in public schools, particularly in vocational training, where hands-on experience is a valuable asset, and where there is a tradition of movement from crafts into teaching. Moreover, these "transfer teachers" could be assisted by volunteers at all levels of instruction. For example, specialists from industry or nearby colleges could teach high school courses in advanced science or math—or police officers could teach courses in civics and driver's education. In point of fact, in many disciplines, teacher shortages in high school stand alongside college faculty gluts. More staff interaction should be encouraged.

The primary impediment to lateral entry and volunteerism in public schools has been teacher militancy on both subjects. We favor the amendment of collective bargaining agreements and state certification requirements so that prospective teachers from outside the system can share their gifts more fully with America's school children. In addition, we note that, in recent years, union militancy regarding "volunteerism" has begun to abate. More and more teachers have come to view volunteer workers as positive resources, whose presence benefits public education as a whole. This trend must continue.

A fourth area where the educational impact of business can and should be more positively felt relates to television. We have found very few educators with a positive image of what television contributes to children and school. Clearly, the medium offers certain advantages—the capacity to distribute information in a vivid way and to help children experience current events over great distances in a very short period of time. But, once past that point, there are severe problems.

As discussed earlier, we live in an age when adults have grown quite distant from children. Inevitably, in the lives of many youngsters, TV characters substitute for adult role models who should be, but aren't, there. And from the standpoint of many parents, there is nothing quite as easy as putting a child in front of a television set, leaving that child there for several hours, then coming back and pretending there has been communication and an exchange of views between parent and child. Many children spend more time watching television than they spend in school. And the content of commercial television is unsatisfactory—bland at best, often highly negative in that it promotes poor values and various types of antisocial behavior—problems compounded by the recent growth of cable television and the video cassette industry.

Children do not have the critical judgment necessary to defend against the onslaught of television. Thus, we must seek to infuse television with positive values that will sustain and encourage the very best in children. But, beyond this, we must realize that television takes youngsters away from reading and social interaction with other children. Moreover, contrary to the mission of education, which seeks to prepare children for active adult roles, watching TV entails being passive and unproductive. The development by American business of more and better educational television programs and networks is a must.

In sum, we endorse a new partnership between America's public schools and its business community. We do not seek an involvement that will negate the need for ample tax dollars in support of education, nor would we replace government sponsorship with that of big business. Moreover, we recognize that there are risks involved. As a consequence of this endeavor, private business will have more influence in shaping school policy than some would like, and a downturn in corporate profits or a change in corporate public relations strategy could have an adverse impact on many school programs. Still, we believe these risks are outweighed by the very clear potential for gain involved.

The need for the business community's commitment to public education cannot be overstated. We hope to encourage a level of corporate involvement unknown since the depression, a commitment by chief executive officers and other business leaders to participate personally in the process of education. Educators need public support. They need other people to assist and guide them. When someone comes in from the outside and contributes in a positive way to teachers and students, it reinforces the meaning of education for us all.

Parents

Other than students, no group has more of an interest in education than the parents of children in school. This makes parents both a power in and an invaluable resource to public schools. Positive parental influences upon education include teaching children to read at an early age, overseeing their homework, and encouraging them to do well in the classroom. No one can doubt the importance of the parents' role. Children have a definite advantage when their parents support them in school. Yet unfortunately, and perhaps tragically, not enough parents know what to do, are willing to do it, or are sufficiently involved. In many cases, parents simply cannot discharge their duties to their children, thus underscoring the need for a school system that aggressively advocates the cause of children.

Recent studies indicate that, during the course of an average school year, only one-third of all parents with children in public school attended a PTA or school board meeting. Almost 40 percent did not have a single conference with any teacher or administrator to discuss their child. Parents in general cede too much power to professional educators in setting standards and goals for their children. This failure to participate in school affairs is particularly true of fathers of children in public school, few of whom attend school functions other than "back to school night." They often act as though educating children were a feminine responsibility. Indeed, other than certain athletic events, neither of the authors of this book has ever attended a public school function open to parents where mothers did not outnumber fathers in attendance. Some interested fathers tell of nights when they were almost alone at an assembly of school mothers.

Parents must understand that they are not professional educators. They do not assign youngsters to classes, or make decisions regarding who teaches what subject. But they should also realize that, outside of family development, formal education is the most important activity that goes on in the life of a child.

We actively seek broader parental participation and input in school. If parents are casual about grades and schoolwork, it encourages children to be casual too. Having said this though, we hasten to add that it is not necessarily a sign of indifference when a parent fails to participate in school programs. Some parents who care a great deal about their children don't get involved because they feel inadequate to the task and insecure in their relationships with professional educators. They themselves are often uneducated and unable to relate to the system. School to them is a complex arena and, rather than be embarrassed by their inadequacies, they stay at home.

These parents must be made to feel welcome in school and, toward that end, educators will have to work very hard. They must develop workshops, panel discussions, and other programs to inform all parents of their responsibilities to school-age children and involve all parents in the process of education. Parents associations should be mandated by all school systems, and they should run programs that bring other parents into school. Once this sort of activity has begun, teachers and administrators will be able to utilize parents more fully in educating each and every child. Just as we ask teachers and other individuals within the system to forego their own special interests in favor of a broader agenda on behalf of children, we demand that parents sacrifice to fulfill the needs of children in school.

Beyond this, two additional points regarding parental involvement in public education should be made, and the first of these deals with power. The individual child should be placed and treated in public schools according to his or her needs, not according to whose parents are the most powerful. We began this book with a very simple message: all children are equal—and therefore public schools cannot promote a strategy that meets the needs of children with concerned, educated parents and, at the same time, pulls the wool over the eyes of parents who don't know any better. Perhaps the most serious abuse of children's rights in the education process comes when school officials make decisions based not on the needs of children, but on parental power. This problem manifests itself in many forms. Indeed, in some school districts, it appears as though classes for the gifted contain more children of gifted parents than gifted children. Just because a child's parents are too unaware to exert pressure does not mean that a child should be denied his or her entitlement to a quality education.

Too many people ignore the issue of equity, yet equity must run through the system as a primary value in our schools. When decisions are made about preferences and zoning, public schools must defend the rights of those without true representation. Very often, political forces don't like this. They prefer to tilt toward those who lobby the hardest or have the most power at the polls. But it is the responsibility of educators to ensure that tilting does not occur. This is the meaning of equality. Entitlements go to all children because they are children. Middle-class children aren't any better; poor children aren't any better; upper-class children aren't any better. They are all equal. Their entitlements run across the board.

Also, and equally important, we have talked about the need to bring parents into the school system. The corollary to that is: lack of parental participation does not mean that educators should throw their hands up in the air and say they can't educate a particular child. All too often, we blame children for their failure; and then, when we get tired of blaming children, we blame the parents for a child's inability to learn. School systems do not need parental involvement for children to perform. If they did, we would never be able to educate orphans. And the fact of the matter is, we do educate orphans— and we can educate children whose parents don't care and don't come to school. Is it easy? No, it's very hard— much harder without parents than with them. But it can be done. If a public school really works, children of parents who don't care can master basic skills as well as the children of parents who are involved. Poor minority children who come from the most disadvantaged of homes can take just as much from school as rich white ones.

4

Toward Better Schools

Quality education is a lifetime process that begins long before the first day of school. It requires effort, discipline, and sometimes pain. In the preceding chapter, we suggested ways in which certain interest groups could improve the day-to-day operation of public schools. To this we now add a few thoughts regarding the structure and organization of public schools.

Effective Schools

The process of education is not an abstract principle. Public schools work effectively in many places because educators know what to do and care about doing it well.

Not many years ago, the literature of effective schooling failed to recognize that student learning depended on what was done in school. Studies focused on factors beyond the control of principals and in-school staff. The condition of school buildings, student-teacher ratios, the number of school library volumes, and the like were considered more important than how teachers taught. Then emphasis shifted to the socioeconomic status of students, and again the success or failure to educate was regarded as largely beyond the control of educators. In recent years, however, scholars and practitioners alike have come to realize that student learning depends on the individual school. And, although no set formula exists, certain characteristics are almost universally shared by effective schools:

1. One of the most tangible and perhaps indispensable characteristics of an effective school is strong administrative leadership. In such schools, the principal is likely to be an assertive instructional leader, willing to assume responsibility for evaluating the fulfillment of basic goals.

2. Effective schools have a climate of expectation and an instructional system in which no child is permitted to slide without notice below minimum levels of achievement. Teachers believe in their students and challenge their students to perform.

3. The atmosphere in an effective school is orderly but not rigid. Order is a value, because without order there can be little learning. Students have little time for "acting out." Discipline is related to the educational task at hand.

4. Student acquisition of basic skills takes precedence over all other activity in an effective school. There is heavy emphasis on reading and mathematics. The entire staff is committed to being instructionally effective, and, when necessary, resources are diverted from other activities to ensure the learning of basic skills.

5. Student progress is regularly monitored and the results used as the basis for instructional programs. Tests are frequently administered to ensure that teachers and administrators remain aware of student achievement in meeting instructional goals.

* * *

There are many individuals with varying responsibilities who contribute to effective schools. In some instances, a strong, assertive principal compels teachers to lift all students to acceptable levels of achievement. Other schools are effective because of an extremely able, dedicated corps of teachers, who are never fully satisfied with their performance and constantly challenge both their students and themselves. These teachers know that there is no such thing as a school that is "holding its own." Either a school is improving, or it is in decline. Still another group of effective schools are influenced by well-organized parents associations that hold teachers, administrators, and ultimately children to the highest standards of performance.

We have the knowledge and experience to educate all students well. And, beyond that, children are capable of learning in many more ways than we know how to teach them. Thus, the real question is one of commitment. Will the education establishment make the effort needed in the next decade to produce more in our public schools?

School as a Bridge to Adulthood

The central task of America's schools is the transmission of basic skills—reading, writing, mathematics, science, social studies, and, in the next decade, computer literacy. But beyond that, schools must prepare children for the assumption of adult roles. This process starts the moment children first enter school. They understand that something is happening to them, something that will tear them away from their parents and force them to function on their own. They cry; they don't want to be there; but a tremendous threshold has been crossed. The children have taken on a measure of independence in preparation for adulthood.

The more of "the real world" that creeps into school, the better prepared children will be to assume the responsibilities of adulthood later on. School is not only a place where reading and science are taught. These subjects are important, but, in the final analysis, schools must do more than teach basic skills. Children must develop the capacity to reason, speak, listen, and think clearly in school. They must learn to use those talents in an intelligent manner, and, toward that end, it is imperative that they be given more things of consequence to do in the classroom.

Chores, an obligation that built character for children in years past, are unfamiliar to students today. We would like chores to be emphasized more than they now are in school. First-grade students who serve as class milk monitors are performing a chore. So are the eighth graders who shelve books in school libraries, and high school seniors who operate a school switchboard for an hour each afternoon. We propose more student involvement in the day-to-day operation of schools through various work and apprentice programs. For example, students could be assigned to assist school maintenance workers on a volunteer basis. Not only would these students be contributing to the school community—they would be learning about basic maintenance, electricity, and plumbing and would experience the satisfaction of performing a job.

The bridge to adulthood would also be better constructed if students were taught the value of attendance in school. The truancy rate in America's public schools is alarming. In some districts, only 60 percent of all upper-grade students come to class. Urban school attendance *averages* in the 80 percent range.

Think about that for a moment! A worker who comes to work 80 percent of the time is an unsatisfactory worker. The average attendance rate for students in urban public schools is not good enough for these students to hold a job. Our students don't even understand the importance of attendance—primarily because too few educators tell them they have to come to school. Instead, teachers and administrators tend to ignore truancy because poor attenders are usually the same students who are "troublemakers" in class. These students never learn that they are important people, that their attendance is something to be valued. Later, though, when dropouts go out into the real world, they don't understand that the license they had to cut classes expired when they got jobs. If they don't show up for work, they will find themselves unemployed.

Public educators can form bridges to adulthood in other ways as well. One small but significant example involves the economics of saving. Up until the 1960s, children were taught the value of saving money in school. Teachers collected nickels and dimes weekly from elementary school children and opened bank accounts for each child. These programs have since been largely abandoned, because "too much paper work" was involved. They should be reinstated because, without them, some children no longer learn a basic economic lesson in school. And if Americans cannot learn basic economics, our savings rate will continue at 4 percent of earnings, compared with much higher rates in other industrialized countries.

Public schools should also encourage independent study courses for students prepared to assume the responsibilities of that freedom. Too often, students misunderstand what education is about. They think it constitutes a set of facts to be given to them rather than their ability to learn. They become wholly dependent on teachers for information and see no reason for the acquisition of knowledge if they haven't "taken the course" in school. But teachers are not going to be watching students once their formal education is at an end, and it is counterproductive to have an educational structure in which the only responsibility a child has is to satisfy the particular needs of a particular teacher at a given time.

Homework is another essential in developing a student's capacity to grow. It teaches children that their responsibility extends beyond the school building and encourages both self-discipline and the ability of students to act on their own. Also, it enables students of lower ability to achieve commensurate with their brighter peers through increased study, and it improves learning as measured by standard test scores. Each school district should have a policy that prescribes a minimum amount of homework for every grade in every school. This policy should ensure that homework is an adjunct to classwork and not seen as mindless drill work or punishment. Moreover, homework should be responsive to a course's curriculum, individualized to help the particular child, carefully explained in advance to every student, and returned to students with constructive criticism once a lesson is done. Properly assigned and corrected daily, homework introduces students to research methodology, libraries, and books other than those read in class. And if students learn to like homework, as many students do, they will begin to read and study on their own. Then they won't need a teacher to tell them to appreciate good books. In sum, homework serves children in many ways, and long after formal instruction has come to an end.

We also believe that schools should offer classes and opportunities that will serve as preparation for careers in military service. This is an unpopular option in some circles, but we do not view the military as an instrument of any one segment of American society. Rather, the military belongs to society as a whole. Military service offers steady employment and, ultimately, additional training and new skills. Given the obligation of schools to maximize options for students, Junior ROTC can be an important program. We add though, that public schools must avoid making military service the primary option for poor and minority students. All students must be introduced to a wide range of blue and white-collar jobs.

In sum, schools have to become places where youngsters practice and prepare for adult roles. Our children are, after all, preparing to be citizens in a democracy. They will be called upon to defend the nation and improve it. They will have to be producers of goods, values, and services, not just consumers. A few thoughts regarding the most practical and efficient way to reach that goal follow.

Students Are Workers

School is a business. Nationwide, public schools spend over $130 billion annually. That's a lot of money. Unfortunately, too much of it is wasted; and one of the reasons it's wasted is that educators see students as recipients of a service. The entire orientation of school is toward providing benefits to student-consumers; and that is a very wrong view of what school is about.

We must stop looking at what resources go into the educational process and begin to focus on what comes out. We must become more absorbed with the product of education—what students learn. Schools must be seen and measured in terms of their output—particularly high schools, whose students are close to adulthood.

Traditional theories regard teachers and administrators as the only education workers in school. This must change. Students must be regarded as productive workers. Teachers must be regarded as managers, those who organize the learning. Schools should be places where children come to work—to learn—and practice adult roles.

In many ways, all students are disadvantaged within the system because they lack two critical elements of power—they can't vote and they can't strike. The absence of these weapons renders them passive and without political or economic power. But a capable educator will communicate to children just how important they are in determining their own success and how much they really can do. Good schooling encourages children to realize the full value of their worth and puts students to work at the task of sustaining themselves. America's schools have engendered many of their own problems by failing to understand that *it is children who are the producers and creators in school.*

Ask any principal how many people he or she has on staff and the answer will be, "I have forty teachers." Maybe janitors and cafeteria workers are counted too. Rarely does a principal say "I have a thousand workers. They are students, who produce an output—their own learning—that brings satisfaction to the community, satisfaction to their parents, and satisfaction to themselves." Yet if a manager comes to realize that his or her work force is multiplied twenty or thirty times, so much more can be attained.

Prevailing views toward teachers can be seen as a further example. All teachers have a college education. Many, if not most, have masters or other graduate school degrees. In few other professions would a person with a masters degree not supervise a number of fellow employees. Yet teachers are thought of as being the lowest workers on an assembly line with no other workers beneath them. And, as a result, they too seldom challenge students to perform.

Teachers are not assembly-line workers. They are managers of what should be a very productive enterprise, and the product of that enterprise is what students learn. Educators must be constantly reminded that they have in their possession a collection of extremely important assets—children—children with skills and the potential to do a good job. This is the perspective we seek to encourage. Teachers are managers of classroom instruction.

Their job is to manage what students learn. Such a theory, if put into practice, would alter the entire relationship that exists today in America's public schools.

The relationship at present is as follows: the principal manages teachers; teachers dole out a service; the students consume. The principal is resented; the teachers are underused; and the potential of students is unrealized. By contrast, an effective model for public education would consider principals as general managers supervising another set of managers. The workers on the assembly line would be the students themselves.

We repeat: schools must focus on what students learn. Yet, in practice, a different focus exists today in most schools. When a principal walks into a classroom to observe instruction, too often emphasis is placed on whether the teacher's lesson begins and ends on time, whether it features all the components of a well-rounded plan, and perhaps whether the window shade is properly drawn. If these criteria are met, the principal is pleased and the model developed in schools of teacher education has been satisfied. But what if the students don't learn? What if the teacher has been talking to a stone wall? In too many instances, it doesn't seem to matter, because the principal has been watching the teacher, not the children.

Public education will never be reformed if we continue to see schools as places where the government dumps loads of money, instead of places where children are called upon to produce and perform. True change will come only when school adminstrators learn to regard their staff resources as encompassing teachers *and students*. And the beauty of regarding students as workers is, from a productive point of view, you can work them very hard. You can work them long hours; you can give them as much homework as you want; and they don't get paid overtime. Also, you can get a very fine product in return.

In sum, too many educators have ignored the ability of students to be workers. They minimize the capacity of children to perform, and this in turn means that they wind up supervising less creative individuals. When children think that work is something they will not encounter until later in life, then those children have been short-changed.

To demonstrate our point, we refer to a particular inner-city school. Two thousand students attended this school and, at times, it seemed as though all two thousand threw paper on the floor. Then a new principal was assigned to the school and decided, "If I can impress on students that this is their workplace, that littered halls are ugly, two thousand students will feel an obligation to pick paper up rather than throw it down. And, if picking up paper becomes a work ethic in school, these same students won't throw paper on the floor at all."

Many principals would have come into the same school, decried the condition of the corridors, and sought to hire two more janitors. The difference in outlook is that, in hiring more janitors, the school would be treating students solely as recipients of a service. Regarding students as producers led to the same end result—a cleaner school—but at less cost and with less work for everyone involved. No one had to pick up paper because, when students were given responsibility and a role, there was less paper to begin with on the floor.

We have to give students more credit for being able to do what is right themselves. Education must be reformed, not only in what we teach children, but in how they are regarded and in what we expect of them. Effective schools move children from consumption to production. They teach children how to do things and do them well.

Accountability and Standards

Even if attitudes toward children change, there will be a need for futher emphasis on standards for public schools:

1. We need standards for educators.
2. We need standards for students.
3. We need ways of measuring a school's performance.
4. Educators must be held accountable for the success or failure of students to perform at required levels.

At present, not enough of the above is happening in our nation's public schools. There are many "require-ments"—teachers must teach five periods a day; certain courses are prerequisite to the attainment of a teaching license. But there are too few standards. And the problem of lax standards for educators is particularly acute.

There is a tale, perhaps allegorical, of a high school teacher who prepared for his initial day on the job by writing his entire lesson out in advance. At the close of the first class, as students were filing out of the room, the teacher approached a shy-looking girl who'd been sitting in the back row and asked, "How did I do?" The child paused to gather her thoughts, then answered, "You read it; you read it badly; and you didn't say nuthin'."

In too many instances, teachers "don't say nuthin' ";
or, when they do, they say it badly. And yet the "requirements" of the job have been met. A large share of the
blame for this situation rests with teachers colleges and
undergraduate schools of education. Overall, with but a
few exceptions, they are the poorest-quality professional
schools in America.

Education, by definition, is conservative. It is designed
to preserve the best of the past and imprint those qualities
upon the future. But teacher training in the United States
is not conservative; it is stagnant. Very often, schools of
education are a dumping ground for the nation's worst
professors and least academically qualified college students. In an age of shrinking enrollment, they will matriculate just about anybody. Thus, although many
high-quality teachers still come into the public school
system, it is often despite their professional preparation
rather than because of it. This dilemma has been exacer-
bated in recent years by the flight of women to other professions. Historically, teaching was one of the few fields
where women were accepted as full participants. Over 70
percent of the public school teachers in the country were
women, although advancement of women to the highest
ranks of the profession did not occur. Women were accepted as teachers, but discriminated against as administrators and organizers. Now, more and more women,
who in years past might have gone into teaching, are becoming doctors, lawyers, and corporate executives. The
result is that teacher candidate ranks are not as impressive
as they were years ago.

The problem is further compounded by the fact that, at
many teachers colleges, the competitive mold is not built

around excellence. Medical schools and law schools train professionals whose livelihood depends at least in part on the strength of their graduate school education. They take advanced courses because their professional standing requires it. By contrast, many teachers take graduate school courses not to learn, but because promotion and salary differentials require additional course hours. They have no interest in difficult courses that demand a great deal of time and effort. They really just want the credits, and the result is a perverse form of reverse competition whereby schools of education compete for students on the basis of how *little* work is demanded in return for course credit. In recent years, even the better schools of education have adopted this practice. In some states, it is now possible to receive a doctoral degree from an accredited university without attending lectures, doing research, taking exams, or writing papers. But the problem is not simply that schools of education enable prospective teachers to take shortcuts in their studies. In many cases, dedicated graduate students confront a curriculum that does not deal with the reality of today's public schools. Even in the most prestigious graduate schools of education, professors seldom examine what is actually happening in local school districts. Instead, their research interests lead them away from practical considerations to exotic, unproductive studies.

Standards for educators must be improved and, toward that end, teachers college curricula should be revised as follows. First, teacher education programs should be better integrated with other university departments and their faculty held to higher standards regarding tenure, promotion, and scholarly activity than is presently the case.

Second, teachers must acquire more subject matter expertise at the undergraduate level. Science teachers must know science; music teachers, music. The job description for a public school teacher, particularly at the high school level, calls for a teacher of subject matter. This requires substantive course work, independent study, and research. Our schools have too many math teachers who are experts in math education instead of math.

Third, teachers colleges should reduce methodological course work and move teacher candidates into classroom settings as student-teachers sooner than now occurs. Every educator who sets foot in a classroom must know what a lesson is, how to command attention, and how to structure a student's classroom experience. But these skills do not require extensive course work or sophisticated techniques, nor should they be studied only in the abstract. Indeed, most university doctoral programs—which are apprenticeships for teaching on the college level—require no courses in teaching methodology at all. Thus, a bizzare situation exists in American education. High school seniors are instructed by men and women who have limited subject matter expertise but a large number of methodology credits. A semester later, as college freshmen, these same students are taught by professors with no education credits whatsoever.

Fourth, there should be new courses in teacher education, focusing on problems that teachers and administrators face in today's public school setting. Additional coursework in business, management, and industrial psychology is a must. For more than a decade, school violence has been cited in public opinion polls and by educators as a major problem, yet no courses on school safety are offered to prospective administrators and teachers in most areas of the country. Here again, there is a need for more.

Also, there is an urgent need to upgrade the textbooks used in public schools. The current trend among educators is to infuse as many facts as possible into students' heads with the least effort possible on the part of the child. Thus, textbooks are written to compete with television and video games, and the notion that children should be lifted to a higher standard by reading material has been largely ignored. Textbooks are now sold on the basis of which one is easiest for the child. We need more challenging textbooks for children. The issue is not whether this should occur, but how.

Standards for *students* in our public school system are also sadly lacking. Indeed, when one considers the end product of public education—the high school graduate—it is clear that public schools constitute the most unregulated business in America. If a bank outlined mortgage and loan terms as vaguely as the meaning of a high school diploma is stated, it would run afoul of banking and consumer protection statutes. An airline can't fly planes at whatever height it chooses or land on runways at whim; federal aviation authorities would have a fit. Yet, within the same public school, two students can receive identical diplomas and, in terms of quality performance, those students may be worlds apart. A manufacturer couldn't pack peas in tin cans with the same disregard for standards that public schools are allowed to exhibit. Imagine a company that puts as many peas as it feels like in a can, labels the can any way it chooses, and is oblivious to the threat of poisoning in the canning process. This is the equivalent of what many public schools do in certifying students as graduates. There is no "truth in packaging"; no certainty that the product moving out reflects even an attendance record. The school attests to the number of classes a student took, but without competency examinations—a relatively new phenomenon—it says little regarding the worth of those classes.

Schools must have standards for students. Educators must challenge children. They must make demands, have high expectations, and be more attentive to rigorous subjects like mathematics and science than is now the case. Obviously, some students are brighter than others; some are more talented; others try harder. But all children must be told what is expected of them and what is required for success. We cannot lie to them about the quality of their work or allow sympathy for their disappointment to conceal their shortcomings. Rather, we must correct those shortcomings, so friends, family members, and employers no longer look at high school graduates and ask, "How did they ever get diplomas?"

Too many schools have incorporated into their philosophy a policy known as "social promotion"—the notion that students should advance from grade to grade regardless of performance; that promotion should be virtually automatic. Social promotion is the system's way of being "nice" to students. It is the ultimate derogation of educational standards. Yet social promotion is supported by those within the system who do not want to be held accountable for students' failure, and ending social promotions will be hard to achieve. In New York City, for example, the Gates Program, designed to end social promotion, has been terminated—not by direct school board policy, but by a lack of implementation. Standards for students have been deemphasized recently, and children who fail have been pushed ahead without adequate preparation for the next grade. Inevitably, as these students find themselves unable to perform at a meaningful level, they will drop out of school.

Students respond to what is expected of them. The more that is reasonably demanded, the more they will produce. Social promotion embodies the most pernicious form of reduced expectations. It tells students that academic performance isn't really important and lets "slow learners" think that their failure to achieve is not a matter of concern. It leads children to believe that they are on "the right track" and doing well enough to satisfy. Only later does a moment of truth come when these children learn that their preferred careers are unattainable.

Social promotions in public schools must end, but a school will do students a grave disservice if it holds them back simply to repeat a year in the same program they have already failed once before. Repeat students must be given a course of study that combines encouragement with well-designed remedial instruction. When students are told they have failed, they must also be told that they can achieve success—but that sense of hope must be built on reality. If it is, and if students who fail are accounted for by the system, it will force educators to improve upon the system so that all "poor learners" are taught basic skills properly.

As for student bodies at large, basic competency examinations are one way of imposing minimum standards and targeting areas where further instruction is necessary. These exams should be based upon a standard curriculum, and that curriculum must be adhered to, be constantly reevaluated, and be capable of changing with the times. Too often, a school district's curriculum requirements are handed down from generation to generation in the manner of a sacred scroll. Such a situation is antithetical to education.

Grades are also important, both as a means of assessment and a motivating factor. Children have a right to know how they are doing, and they should be graded as often as necessary to accomplish that end. But grades must be accompanied by common sense and honesty. Students at one elementary school were victimized by a system based on grades of "satisfactory" and "unsatisfactory." For students whose performance was unsatisfactory but showed improvement, there was an intermediate grade of "improving." However, a problem developed when "improving" became the intermediate grade in every sense. Students who had performed well early in the year but then began to slip found themselves dropping from "S" to "I." Yet they were not in any sense "improving." And parents—as well as many students—had trouble understanding what the grades meant. A "nice" explanation grounded on the unrealistic optimism that things are always getting better was used rather than a more accurate grade of "needs improvement."

Grades are an important measure of quality for students. Report cards with clearly defined grades such as numbers or letters should be issued a minimum of four times annually—evenly spaced, the first time after students have experienced a period of adjustment to the new school year. These grades should be based on written examinations and classroom performance. A great deal of effort must go into the grading process to guarantee close correspondence between teaching and instruction and ensure that grades given to students are fair. Moreover, examination papers should be reviewed by teachers and students together so that tests become instruments for learning—not just a means of evaluation. Where possible, report cards should be given directly by teachers to parents. But quality measures should not be restricted to students and staff. They are also necessary to gauge the *overall performance of schools* and, at present, there are very few such systems of measurement in use.

Every person in this country who has an interest in public education ought to ask, "What are public schools doing for our children? Be specific!" What are the average scores for students taking basic competency and college entrance examinations? What percentage of students passed these tests? How many students are attending high school on a regular basis? How many students are involved in extracurricular activities or school government? What percentage of graduates are going on to college? To a job? When these questions are asked, there should be answers readily available from school districts.

Often, educators don't like these questions. They feel that the data gathered becomes an instrument for evaluating them, and they don't want to be evaluated by the performance of their students. Yet that is precisely how educators should be evaluated. Not that numbers are infallible; they're not. Statistics rarely tell the whole truth and sometimes lie. Keep potential dropouts in school, and average reading scores may decline even though more learning is taking place. But intelligent evaluation can overcome the deficiencies inherent in statistics. And as educators grow more accustomed to evaluating and sharing these indicators of pupil performance with the public, they will become less defensive in explaining how well individual schools are performing.

We need ways of measuring school performance—the sum total of student report cards. And, from there, educators must move on to a host of questions regarding school management: How much money can be saved by ordering textbooks jointly with another district? How efficient is the design of a given school building? What are food costs in the school lunch program? How many miles do school buses travel half empty? What *should* it cost to educate a student?

At present, our data systems are primitive, and there are no adequate figures regarding the most cost-efficient way to give large numbers of children a quality education. Little research has been done on comparative school costs or comparative school performance, and almost always the issue is avoided by the education establishment. Some rough measures have been taken, but educators really don't know how educational costs and the educational product of school systems in other parts of the country compare with their own. Schools are so localized and use information so much for their own purposes that educators have failed to establish a reliable data bank that would enable them to measure costs against performance. The data that would be considered essential in running an ordinary business are lacking within public school systems. Indeed, those few data requirements that do exist within schools are generally designed to determine compliance with already authorized budgets and specially funded programs. There are no data requirements to assist in prospective decisions. It is almost as though educators are afraid to study the relationship between cost and quality for fear that, given entrenched interests, the resulting data could not be acted upon.

This neglect must end. And the way to end it is to hold educators accountable for the success or failure of students to perform in school at levels justifiable by a community's financial input. To date, public schools have been far too wasteful in managing resources. There's a tradition in education that, if you spend a dollar and it doesn't work, you should spend two dollars; and not only that, you should give those two dollars to the same person who couldn't do the job with only one. In many cases, school districts have refused to consider new management techniques and resisted basic good business management. Some educators seem to think that government should pay them to continue producing a product, even though the product doesn't work. Indeed, when government gives out remedial education grants today, those grants are distributed on the basis of need. Who are the most needy? The most needy are students who have been in the system for eight or ten years and still haven't learned. Funds are distributed on the basis of jobs not done. Extra dollars are given to educators who have often showed no ability to handle their jobs properly in the past. Indeed, many educators—far too many—find that their federal grants are cut once they have brought their students up from a level of inadequate performance to satisfactory standards. The financial incentives actually run against achievement in school. We submit that before public school systems get additional financial aid, which many of them need desperately, they be required to institute programs that guarantee accountability. That is, educators must be held responsible for the performance of their students. The failure to achieve success over a period of time should be penalized, not rewarded.

At present, there is too little at stake for educators in whether or not school systems work. Accountability, with appropriate rewards and sanctions, would change this. Let's focus on teachers for a moment. At present, two teachers can begin at the same school on the same day. One might be a brilliant teacher, the other barely satisfactory. At the end of ten years, these teachers will have substantially similar duties and be making substantially similar salaries. Their level of pay will be determined by how long they have taught and, to a degree, by how many graduate school courses they have taken—not by how well they teach or which teacher better serves the needs of children.

There has to be room within the system to reward the teacher who is doing a better job. School systems cannot talk about promoting excellence among children and fail to reward excellence on the part of teachers. We cannot run school systems that evaluate students but are incapable of evaluating adults. If schools have a mechanism for saying, "These students are achieving; they're in the top 10 percent of the class," a similar mechanism must be found to differentiate between teachers. It might be hard, but it would be well worth the effort. Politics aside, most people know who the best teachers are. The students know; the administrators know; the teachers know. And, usually, their judgment is the same.

The principle of accountability demands that union contracts and school district practice be reformed so that teachers are no longer paid strictly on the basis of seniority, and that annual salary increases are no longer given on an automatic basis. Generally, experienced teachers are entitled to a greater salary than inexperienced ones. By virtue of their experience, they are likely to have developed additional skills and made significant contributions to the school community. But there are great differences in ability among teachers, and true accountability will never be taken seriously until it is accompanied by financial incentives. Not even teachers—as dedicated and devoted as they are—are motivated purely by professionalism. Teachers who give out grades to students should be able to understand that they too can be graded. Good teachers deserve to earn something more—because they are good.

We propose merit pay for teachers in the form of annual bonuses—equal to approximately 10 percent of their salary—to particularly deserving instructors. These bonuses should be based on productivity measured in terms of a school's educational goals. Merit pay should *not* be built into a teacher's salary base. It is a bonus, to be earned one year at a time. Similar rewards could be offered to school principals and other administrators based on the overall performance of their schools.

Merit pay will cost more. We recognize that. Costs are bound to go up in any school system that has reform built into it. To a degree, attracting better teachers will cost money. Improved science laboratories and computer capability will cost money. Longer school days and a longer school year—measures proposed by many educators—

will cost money. There simply is no way around the fact that education is a costly business. But before all of the items mentioned above are put into place, the principle of accountability requires that their cost be matched with projected results. Before massive expenditures are earmarked for public education, educators must demonstrate that they are willing to be bound by realistic standards of productivity. If schools are to get more dollars, what will they produce? What will happen to reading scores? What about the school dropout rate? And who, if anyone, will lose his or her job if satisfactory results are not achieved? The upgrading of standards will take time to accomplish. It won't be enough for state policy makers simply to announce a new set of guidelines. Rather, the entire culture of schools will have to be brought to the point where standards are understood, valued, implemented, and enforced. Only then—and only when student test results show significant improvement both in grade scores and the participation level of eligible students—should educators be satisfied.

We get angry when we see a school that educates poorly—and several miles away there is another school with the same amount of public funding and a similar student body that is educating beautifully. We get angry when educators fail to remember that teaching leads to learning, and if children aren't learning, then schools are part of the problem. Students can learn far more than they are currently being asked to learn. We have seen them do more. They can be pushed by quality teaching and higher expectations, by a demand for standards and a sense of accountability on the part of educators.

A Sense of Community

In the main, we have discussed standards and accountability in terms of basic skills, but educators must recognize a broader mission. Public schools are committed to universal education. As part of this undertaking, there must be an effort to introduce a common culture and develop a sense of community within each school.

Every school is a small social system. And within this system, students must be taught the value of citizenship and community participation. Many educators neglect this responsibility. They see themselves as teachers of English or teachers of science. They are not. They are teachers of children, and every educator must understand that his or her obligation extends beyond the teaching of subject matter. They must teach the whole child and address needs that are unmet by a formal curriculum. They must be assertive in their dealings with students and teach children the meaning of responsibility, self-worth, right and wrong. They must guide students in the matter of how fellow students should be treated and how they as individuals can express themselves.

One way in which a sense of community can be instilled is through peer tutoring. In single-room schoolhouses decades ago, older students taught and cared for younger ones. Instructional roles were shared. Peer tutoring has fallen out of fashion since then, but its potential for good remains. It is capable of encouraging children to think of themselves as teachers as well as learners. It can make them feel useful and remind them at an early age that they have responsibilities to others. It can draw out the shy, reluctant youngster who is worried about relations with colleagues and not yet comfortable with them. We cite the example of a Korean child in high school who spoke no English and was lost in school. Another Korean student—previously a very shy boy—began to serve as his interpreter. Soon both students had been transformed. The first child had become an active learner. And the second student, in addition to discharging a very important role, had reinforced his own sense of competence and dignity.

Extracurricular activities are also important in developing a school community. Too often, nonacademic pursuits are sacrificed by schools in an effort to balance budgets and improve strictly academic standards. However, these activities are exceedingly important to the quality of life in school. Glee clubs, debate teams, drama groups, and similar activities broaden horizons and give students a sense that they belong. School athletic programs can further the same goal. Regular gym classes and intramural competition engender camaraderie and give students who are not academically gifted the chance to lead and excel. Sports in general teach children how to win, how to accept defeat, and how to work with others toward a common end. Spectator sports, which are the focus of interschool rivalries, can involve an entire school. At their best, these rivalries go beyond the issue of winning or losing. They foster school spirit, sportsmanship, and more.

All too often though, schools fail athletically gifted students by not making the academic demands of them that are made upon students with lesser athletic skills. We are strong proponents of school athletic programs. However, we believe that the primary mission of education is to teach subject matter content and basic skills. Therefore, we would bar students from participation in interschool athletic programs unless those students fulfill the normal requirements of the school. The issue is one of standards and the application of standards in an equal manner. A student who fails to make satisfactory progress toward a diploma is not a satisfactory student. And regardless of how important that student may be to the community's desire to "win," his classroom performance should be priority number one.

Declaring a student academically ineligible to participate on a school team is not done to punish the youngster. Rather, it is done with the hope and expectation that, by strengthening academic standards, educators will encourage students to work harder until their academic deficiencies are cured. Rules on attendance, rules on conduct, rules on classroom performance—all are important in countering the tendency of some students to go in the wrong direction. These rules are not negative. They do not hurt children when enforced from a conscientious, caring perspective. The rules that hurt children are the ones that surprise them, the ones that let them play football for three years while flunking courses. For three years, the student is happy. Then he's told he's not graduating because he has no basic skills, and he's not happy anymore.

Three years of deluding a child into the belief that he's making satisfactory progress toward a diploma when he's not makes an educator a liar. We cannot lie to our children. We must make certain that students understand they are in school to acquire basic skills and knowledge preparatory to adulthood. It is only within this context that extracurricular activities achieve full value.

Another item that impacts on school as a community is tracking, a practice which puts students in classes based on their achievement and potential academic ability. We believe in tracking. No school system can operate without some differentiation in the ability of its students, and the notion that tracking is bad simply because it categorizes students is nonsense. Children understand and accept classification. They know who's in first place in baseball. They know which basketball team is in last place. Every time they play ball, they know that half of them are going to lose, but it doesn't stop them from having a good time. Children can live with being less than first, so long as it is clear that being less than first does not diminish them as individuals or deprive them of hope.

Tracking should begin as soon as the differentiation in student ability and performance is measurable and can be put to good use. However, it is essential that schools look beyond superficial standards in determining tracks. The tendency in education for the gifted is to focus on those children who are easiest to teach and have scored well on a single IQ test or achievement examination. If tracking is to be truly successful, definitions of "academically gifted" must be broader than this. Also, tracking should not penalize late bloomers by locking children in place. Groupings must be fluid enough to permit advancement from one level to another, so that student achievement is stimulated and no group is isolated from the rest of the school community.

Tracking can, if poorly implemented, have several drawbacks. Students respond to what is expected of them.

The more that is reasonably demanded, the more they will produce. If a student is perceived as a "slow learner," called upon less frequently in class, and assigned less demanding work, that student will lower his or her own self-expectations and produce far less than would otherwise be the case. Therefore, schools must make sure that tracking does not become a way of giving up on children. Nor can educators forget that definitions of gifted vary within a school community. Some students are marvelously talented with their hands. Others are particularly good in music. The smartest student is not always the best, the most valuable, or the most giving. Educators must respect every child's talents. If they do, tracking can contribute to a school's sense of community.

Extended use of school facilities—and, in particular, greater use of school buildings after regular school hours —can also contribute to meeting students' needs. Here, we begin with simple building maintenance. In many school districts, particularly urban ones, deferred maintenance has left classrooms in a state of disrepair. No responsible business would give its physical plant the kind of limited support often evident in school buildings. Broken windows and leaking roofs are not an environment conducive to learning. Beyond this, we believe that schools should be open year-round and till the end of each day— not for increased formal instruction, but for additional student activity. Most schools shut down on weekends, for holiday vacations, and for two months each summer. Few other businesses close their doors for 50 percent of every year. School buildings have to be utilized on a more cost-efficient basis. Moreover, students should not be forced to leave school simply because it is three o'clock and the traditional school day is over. School should be a place where students can stay until there is another appropriate place for them to go. Street corners, discos, and video-game arcades should get strong competition from institutions that serve children.

The use—or misuse—of school libraries is an example in point. When are school libraries open? When class is in session. When are school libraries closed? After school, when students might use them. Library hours should be expanded so they are available on weekends, after school, and during the evening. They should be places of activity; homes away from home, where children can spend as many hours as possible reading and studying. The same holds true for public libraries. In many areas of the country, budget cutbacks have curtailed library hours and, in some instances, resulted in the closing of branch libraries. The result is that public libraries are often open when school is open and closed when school is closed—and cannot possibly serve children. Even as television takes children away from books, reduced access to libraries further contributes to the malaise.

However, although we favor greater use of school facilities than is presently the case, we do not think that longer class hours, as proposed by many educators, are an appropriate remedy. Most students already have a full day. They get up early to come to school; they work in class, do homework, baby-sit for siblings, and hold down weekend jobs. They have structured their lives in a way that keeps them busy from the time they wake up until they go to bed, and they don't need to sit in class for an additional two hours every day. They may need additional facilities. They may need help in getting a job; or a library that is open so they have a place to study. But they do not need longer school hours and more formal instruction in basic skills. The issue is not how much time is spent in class. It is how time in and out of class is spent.

Schools can also play an invaluable role with regard to health care and health education for all children. For example, we would like to see medical and dental examinations become common in schools again. Fifty years ago, dental clinics were often found in urban schools. Now they aren't—primarily because methods of treatment have become so sophisticated that public schools can't afford the equipment demanded by clinicians. In the 1930s, a dentist would come in, look at a child's mouth, and at least determine whether there was something visibly wrong. Today, because of technological advances in dentistry, there are elaborate clinics with all sorts of sophisticated equipment located in hospital settings. But for children who are not being examined, this is the equivalent of no clinic at all. Dental examinations should take place where the children are, and that is in school. A simple preliminary diagnosis might not evaluate everything that is wrong with a child's teeth, but, from the standpoint of the child, it is better than no examination— which is what many children are getting now.

Health education should also be a staple in school. This includes teaching children about the dangers of smoking and advising them on proper nutrition, personal hygiene, and sexual conduct. Given contemporary mores, the latter area is of particular importance. In an age when fewer and fewer youngsters receive guidance at home, the role of schools in educating students about sex cannot be overlooked. The controversy over this issue stems largely from the fear of indoctrination that many parents hold. These parents do not realize that children today are too aware of sex and, at the same time, too uninformed.

Drug education is another area ripe for school intervention. Too often, when a child is on drugs, it is seen by educators as a discipline problem. The student isn't doing what he's supposed to do; he's violating the rules. More helpful would be a perspective that says the child is on a road he shouldn't be on; that he is in trouble and needs help.

Schools must confront the issue of drug abuse directly. There must be a planned curriculum that acknowledges the presence of drugs and formulates strategies as to how to deal with the situation. Teachers must learn the symptoms of drug abuse and how to identify students who have fallen victim. There must be counseling and an effort to involve home influences in treatment whenever possible. Also, some funds earmarked for drug treatment should be redirected to the prevention of drug problems. However, the key to prevention is for educators to develop closer ties to children and maintain more of a presence in their lives than is presently the case. And this, in turn, highlights the need for an extended school setting. Students who are in trouble with drugs tend to be children who are not absorbed in more productive pursuits. And one way of ameliorating the situation is to give these students more to do. Toward this end, school facilities should be available throughout the day into early evening. Students playing basketball in the school gym or listening to records in the cafeteria are far less likely to get into trouble than students wandering the streets or sitting alone at home. Even unsupervised activity in school is preferable to time spent in a less desirable environment. Fostering a sense of community in school will decrease student drug abuse. And it will reduce other problems as well.

One of the most vexing nemeses faced by educators is "the disruptive child," Can promoting community values make a difference here? We believe it can. Generally speaking, children in school are not looking for trouble. If they were, they'd go elsewhere, where they can't be as easily identified and readily sanctioned. A child who is unwilling to abide by school standards simply won't come to school. It's not as though attendance rates are so high and truants pursued with such vigor that school participation is compelled.

Thus, in most instances, students lean toward proper behavior simply by virtue of the fact that they are in class. And when problems exist, it is often a consequence of some failing within the school. In this regard, we note that disruptive students generally come in groups. Very rarely does a public school have just two or three students in constant need of discipline. In a well-run school, disruptive students stand out. Only in poorly run schools is disruption epidemic, and usually it is because the school does not provide students with a full and constructive instructional schedule. Children with a lot to do are likely to be productively engaged. Students walking unattended through corridors during "free" periods are not.

Disruptive children should be given counseling and, when necessary, placed under observation by a school therapist or other counselor. Suspension should be regarded as a last resort. Too many educators think that, when a student does something wrong, he or she should be suspended. But assume for a moment that a factory worker does something wrong. It would hardly make sense for the business to give that worker a vacation, five days off. And yet schools do that. They suspend disruptive students and, by doing so, encourage them to drop out. They lose the child and, as a result, all society loses that child's potential for productivity as a worker. It is far better to put a disruptive child to work cleaning graffiti from school walls and scrubbing floors than to write that child off as incorrigible.

We add that corporal punishment as a form of discipline is wholly inappropriate. It's unnecessary; it sets a bad example; and it accomplishes nothing. Teachers who are unable to control students without physical coercion are in the wrong profession.

Obviously, there are conflicting views regarding the creation of certain community values in school. Many people feel that a moment of silence or prayer at the beginning of the school day is desirable to establish a sense of respect and order. However, we do not believe that prayer is essential to reflection and meditation in an academic setting. The battle has been waged, courts have made their decision, and it is highly divisive to fight the same battle all over again simply to remind students of a judicial ruling that certain adults don't like. There are many ways that students can be encouraged to focus on values and responsibility without turning the matter into a constitutional struggle.

We also believe that the same lunch should be provided free of charge to all children in public school. At present, poor children get lunch for free. Middle and upper-class children pay for lunch or bring their own. This does not build a sense of community. Rather, it serves to remind students of the difference between them. That's not the way textbooks are distributed. Students don't pay for instructional material based on family income. All texts are provided free of charge. The justification for spending public funds on education is that schools are an instrument of democracy. Lunch has become an accepted part of school, and it should not remind children daily of the disparity that exists between rich and poor.

The promotion of community values also requires that schools reach out beyond their walls. Too many people in America today regard good citizenship as passé and approach their obligations to society in a casual way or not at all. Students should be encouraged to work as volunteers in hospitals and nursing homes. They should be made to understand that they are responsible to give; that they are citizens with citizenship roles. Children must be taught what community values are all about. They can be; and they are. Public school children in the City of New York played a major role in that city's successful water conservation effort several years ago. Through school-implemented programs, students had a profound effect on the way in which all New Yorkers used water. Indeed, one hundred years ago, it was schoolchildren whose pennies helped pay for the erection of the Statue of Liberty in New York Bay.

Similarly, the community at large must be brought into public schools. Every public school should have an alumni association that encourages graduates to repay some of what they were given by that school. Volunteer workers can perform useful roles in school libraries and extracurricular activity programs. Remedial education for adults who have failed to develop basic skills would represent an important link between school and community, as would opening school cafeterias to senior citizens after student lunch hours.

The measures we suggest cannot be accomplished overnight. Educational institutions evolve slowly, and we understand that there are limits to America's capacity to finance reform. However, much of what we propose is modest in cost. Educational capacity can be expanded through proper administration and care. Our schools can do a better job for children if we demand more. Teachers can do more; administrators can do more. And they must, because our children need more from school today than ever before.

5

With Renewed Spirit

We began this book by acknowledging a problem: that the American people have turned away from their faith in public schools. This loss of faith is a tragedy because, in the end, it is public education that best exemplifies what America is about. Public education, more than any other institution, has integrated rich with poor and black with white. It has provided the technology and human capital that made America's economy the strongest in the world. When we talk of public schools, we are talking about nation building. And, in many ways, current skepticism toward public education reflects our loss of confidence as a nation.

Still, there remains a great deal in our public school system to emulate and be proud of. The average American advances to a level of literacy and competence that few humans on this planet ever match. It is only because we are in this time and in this nation that the accomplishment does not seem remarkable. By and large, the people who run our schools do care about children. And many educators properly recognize that today's schoolchildren are America's most valuable resources.

What we must do, then, is stop looking at our public schools as a problem and start looking to them for solutions. We must turn away from the notion that schools are places where children are stored for a while and realize that education holds the key to social, political, and economic development, both on an individual and a national level. We must not allow any segment of our society to remain illiterate. Universal literacy among children of the rich is proof enough that it can occur among children of the poor. And if universal literacy is truly to be a national goal, we cannot be content with educating students currently in school. We must reach out and recapture those who have dropped out as well. We must push and prod every child to the attainment of excellence.

No one model can explain school effectiveness. There is no "best way" for children to learn. However, in the preceding pages, we have identified certain factors that we believe can contribute to better public schools. Foremost among these is recognition of the following:

1. All children can learn. All children are equal. It is the responsibility of the public school system to promote learning and equality among all children.

2. The central task of America's public schools is the transmission of basic skills and the preparation of children to assume adult roles. Schools must serve as bridges to adulthood and focus on what children are capable of achieving after they leave school.

3. Many students come to school with enormous needs and without clear-cut moral values. It is school that must fill the void. Schools must teach children the meaning of responsibility and self-worth and encourage students to discover the differences between right and wrong. They must offer services that used to be provided by families and other community outlets.

4. Students are producers, not consumers. They must be regarded as productive workers, whose attendance and output are valued by others and themselves. Teachers are managers of student instruction.

5. No single individual in a given school is as important as the principal, who must assume responsibility for setting standards and evaluating the achievement of basic goals. Principals must be given greater authority than is presently the case and held to greater account.

6. School superintendents should have a philosophy of education and make that philosophy the basis for administration. They must understand business management, be advocates for children, and lead by example.

7. The primary role of school boards is the development of a district policy that emphasizes choices for parents, entitlements to children, and standards of accountability. Once this policy is determined, implementation should be left to the superintendent of schools.

8. The most important responsibility of the federal government in education is the enforcement of individual rights. Beyond that, the federal government should maintain a leadership position in the formulation of national education policy and step into areas with financial support where there is a critical national need or shortage. However, whenever possible, educational issues should be dealt with at a local level.

9. Effective schools are characterized by a climate of expectation. They are staffed by teachers who believe in children and in the ability of children to master basic

skills. Students must be tested, and when they fall below expected levels of achievement, they should not be promoted until their skills improve.

10. In an effective school, the atmosphere is orderly, but not rigid. Order must be a primary value because, without order, little learning can occur.

11. Not enough is being done in public schools to improve the performance of teachers. A system of rewards must be developed to compensate those teachers who serve students best, and the promotion of teachers to supervisory positions must be based on merit. Teachers owe more to students than the requirements of a union contract.

12. Schools must develop mechanisms for involving outsiders in the work of schools. This requires a partnership and regular patterns of communication with the business community, parents, alumni, political leaders, and representatives of special interest organizations.

13. We need standards for educators. We need standards for students. We need reliable ways of measuring a school's performance. Educators must be held accountable for the success or failure of students to perform at required levels. Toward these ends, state departments of education should set minimum student competency standards as a prerequisite to promotion and receipt of a high school diploma as well as standards for the employment of teachers and other professionals within the public school system.

14. Real reform of public education must be promoted by people outside the education establishment—parents, state leaders, and America's business community. And it

must concentrate on what schools are to accomplish, not what they are to spend.

15. The key to student learning is what goes on in school, not outside it.

Let us end then, where we began—with children. All children want to feel special. They want attention. They want to be noticed. They cannot be treated as numbers or automatons. Public schools must appeal to every child as an individual possessed of special talents. Our schools must become places of hope; places where help is available; where the special qualities of children are nourished and excellence grows.

Children without hope, like gardens without sunlight, are sad to behold. Students without hope cannot learn. They cannot see accomplishments and success in their future. They see what is ugly; they experience despair. They run from responsibility and strike out at others. History will not forgive our failure to educate these children. It will not accept the excuse that they were too black, or too poor; or that we as a people lacked the knowledge and material resources to properly do the job.

Let history record that, in this generation, America rededicated itself to the task and privilege of educating its children—and that we did so in the context of truth, hope, and justice; in the spirit of love.